All Are Welcome:
Inclusive Service Delivery in Catholic Schools

CATHOLIC EDUCATION STUDIES DIVISION

Alliance for Catholic Education Press
at the University of Notre Dame

All Are Welcome:
Inclusive Service Delivery in Catholic Schools

Martin K. Scanlan

ALLIANCE FOR CATHOLIC EDUCATION PRESS
at the University of Notre Dame

Notre Dame, Indiana

*To all families who have felt unwelcome by Catholic schools.
My prayer is that your efforts to knock on our doors
and break barriers to inclusion are transforming us all.*

Alliance for Catholic Education Press
at the University of Notre Dame
158 I.E.I. Building
Notre Dame, IN 46556
http://www.nd.edu/~acepress

ISBN: 978-0-9819501-4-3

Text design by Julie Wernick Dallavis
Cover photograph and design by Mary Jo Adams Kocovski

"All Are Welcome" lyrics by Marty Haugen
Copyright © 1994 by GIA Publications, Inc.
7404 S. Mason Ave., Chicago, IL 60638
www.giamusic.com   800.442.1358
All rights reserved. Used by permission.

Library of Congress Cataloging-in-Publication Data

Scanlan, Martin K., 1970-
   All are welcome : inclusive service delivery in Catholic schools / Martin K. Scanlan.
      p. cm.
   Includes bibliographical references.
   Summary: "Provides theoretical and practical guidance for Catholic school leaders seeking to
more effectively provide integrated and comprehensive services to all students"--Provided by
publisher.
   ISBN 978-0-9819501-4-3 (pbk. : alk. paper)
   1. Catholic schools. 2. Inclusive education. 3. Students with social disabilities. 4. Main-
streaming in education. I. Title.

   LC473.S23 2009
   371.9'046--dc22
                              2009012949

This book was printed on acid-free paper.

Printed in the United States of America.

Table of Contents

Acknowledgments

I am grateful for the support of many individuals who supported me in writing this monograph. Dr. Colleen Capper, who has been my core mentor and guide, pushes my understanding of service delivery systems and equity for all students. Elise Frattura is an important mentor and colleague in my formation as well. Colleen and Elise are pioneers in articulating the model of integrated, comprehensive service delivery, and I am indebted to them for their insight and guidance through the years. My colleagues in the Department of Educational Policy and Leadership in the College of Education at Marquette University are invaluable, providing encouragement to keep me going and critical voices to keep me thinking. In a special way I am indebted to Ed O'Sullivan, my research assistant, for lending a watchful eye over multiple drafts. I also thank Julie Dallavis and Fr. Ronald Nuzzi at the University of Notre Dame for their critical feedback and guidance. I wish to acknowledge the educators in Catholic elementary and high schools with whom I continue to work through my research, teaching, and service. It is my privilege to join you in our common cause of improving Catholic schools for all students. Finally, I thank my family, Melissa, Nico, Lucas, and Clara, for all their love and laughter.

Introduction

Catholic social teaching compels Catholic schools to include and serve traditionally marginalized students, including students in poverty, those with special needs, and English language learners. Over the past half-century Catholic schools have attempted to be inclusive toward students in poverty. However, during this same period these have largely failed to craft service delivery systems for students with special needs and English language learners. Thus, while attending to barriers imposed by poverty, they struggle to ameliorate barriers imposed by disabilities, exceptionalities, and linguistic differences. This monograph provides theoretical and practical guidance for Catholic school leaders seeking to more effectively provide integrated and comprehensive services to all students.

> Let us build a house where love can dwell
> And all can safely live,
> A place where saints and children tell
> How hearts learn to forgive.
>
> Built of hopes and dreams and visions,
> Rock of faith and vault of grace;
> Here the love of Christ shall end divisions;
> All are welcome, all are welcome,
> All are welcome in this place. (Haugen, 1994)

These lyrics are familiar to many Catholics. Haugen's (1994) chorus, "All are welcome in this place," captures the aspiration of the faith to accept all comers. This commitment to community, this instinct to include, is a core Catholic value. Too often, however, the reality in our Catholic schools falls short of this espoused ideal. Catholic school educators struggle to reduce barriers to students across multiple dimensions of diversity. Teachers lack comfort in welcoming students and families who lack proficiency in English. Principals are unsure of how to develop the school's capacity to meet students' special needs. Boards and dioceses are ineffective in generating funding structures that make the schools widely accessible to families living in poverty. Whole school communities have not successfully built relationships across racial, ethnic, and cultural lines, inhibiting their appeal within increasingly

1

pluralistic communities. This book is dedicated to help Catholic school educators more effectively enact the fundamental Catholic value of which they sing, to welcome all.

The larger field of education, in which Catholic schools are nested, wrestles with this pursuit of social justice education. Social justice education focuses on ameliorating marginalization in schools (Theoharis, 2007). All schools can both promote and inhibit social justice education. Schools inhibit social justice when they ignore or perpetuate inequitable education of certain pools of students (Berliner, 2005; Ferri & Connor, 2005; Losen & Welner, 2001; Orfield & Lee, 2005). Literature on social justice education describes how schools can serve traditionally marginalized students, typically identified as students in poverty, of color, with limited English proficiency (R. S. Johnson, 2002; Lopez, 2001; Lopez, Scribner, & Mahitivanichcha, 2001; McLeskey & Waldron, 2000; Scheurich & Skrla, 2003; Smith-Maddox & Wheelock, 1995; Thomas & Collier, 2001; Tomlinson & Allan, 2000) and students with disabilities (Brotherson, Sheriff, Milburn, & Schertz, 2001; Capper, Frattura, & Keyes, 2000; Durtschi, 2005; Frattura & Capper, 2007a; Praisner, 2003; Rea, McLaughlin, & Walther-Thomas, 2002). To promote social justice, Cambron-McCabe and McCarthy (2005) assert, educators must "engage in critical analysis of conditions that have perpetuated historical inequities in schools and…work to change institutional structures and culture" (p. 202).

Within this broad field of education, Catholic schools can serve a distinct role in social justice education. First, as we will explore in chapter 2, the pursuit of social justice education lies at the heart of the Catholic identity of Catholic schools. Second, this pursuit within Catholic schools serves the common good. In other words, Catholic schools can and do promote social justice as part of their core identity, and in doing so, they not only serve their Catholic mission, but serve the broader field of education and the larger civic community. On one hand, to the degree that they enact policies and practices that reflect Catholic social teaching, emphasizing human dignity, the common good, and a preferential option for the marginalized, Catholic schools promote social justice. On the other hand, to the degree that Catholic schools effectively serve traditionally marginalized students, these students are more equitably distributed across educational sectors. Thus, public schools benefit when Catholic schools effectively welcome traditionally marginalized students.

While the pursuit of social justice is integral to the Catholic identity of Catholic schools, educators in the field of Catholic education are well served by an evenhanded perspective on the strengths and weaknesses of their schools in promoting social justice education. Like all private schools, Catholic schools tend to be more exclusionary than schools in the public sector (Alt & Peter, 2002; Belfield, 2003; Broughman & Swaim, 2006; National Center for Education Statistics, 2002). Families select to enroll their children in private schools, and by design, private schools have considerable discretion in accepting or denying admission requests (Alt & Peter, 2002). Underdeveloped special education service delivery models, reliance on tuition, and other factors contribute to private schools enrolling proportionately fewer traditionally marginalized students, ranging from low socioeconomic status, to students of color, to students with limited English proficiency, to students with disabilities or at risk for disabilities (Alt & Peter, 2002; Broughman & Swaim, 2006). Exceptions to this trend include select private schools that embrace a specific mission, such as schools for students with disabilities or schools that by design seek to serve students in poverty (Salisbury, 2003). Generally speaking, however, private schools tend to prioritize the private interests of their constituents over the public good.

Although Catholic schools reflect some of these exclusionary tendencies common to all private schools, they also present a more complex picture. Catholic schools are more heterogeneous than most of their private sector counterparts. For instance, while less than half (49.5%) of private schools serve students in poverty, nearly 7 in 10 (68.9%) of Catholic schools do (Alt & Peter, 2002). Nationally, Catholic schools are also more diverse across race and ethnicity than other private sector schools (Alt & Peter). Nearly 25% of total Catholic school enrollment are students of color. Furthermore, 21.4% of Catholic schools had greater than 50% students of color, compared to only 15% for other religious schools (Alt & Peter). The religious mission that Catholic schools espouse pressures them to reach out to traditionally marginalized students (Grace, 2002; Jacobs, 1998c).

Evidence suggests that Catholic schools do reflect social justice education in several ways. From their roots in the early 1800s through the 1960s, Catholic schools in the United States were inclusive of Catholic students in poverty and from immigrant communities (Augenstein, 2003; Hunt, 2000; McGreevy, 2003; Moore, 2003). A range of research has shown them to have strong educational outcomes for students in poverty and students of color, especially in recent decades (Alt & Peter, 2002; Bryk, 2000; Bryk, Lee, & Holland, 1993; Coons, 1997; Hoffer, 2000; Hoffer, Greeley, & Coleman, 1985; Lee, Chow-Hoy, Burkam, Geverdt, & Smerdon, 1998; McEwan, 2000; Sander, 1996, 2001). Regarding socioeconomic status, while research indicates that access to Catholic schools for students in poverty has substantially declined (Baker & Riordan, 1998, 1999), several examples are emerging of significant efforts to confront this problem (Finn & Petrilli, 2008; Hamilton, 2008a; O'Keefe & Evans, 2004; O'Keefe et al., 2004). Regarding race and ethnicity, while school segregation by race and ethnicity persists nationally (Orfield & Lee, 2005), some evidence suggests that Catholic schools are more likely to provide groupings of students that are heterogeneous across these dimensions (Greene, Peterson, & Du, 1998). Educational achievement appears more equitably distributed by social class, race, and ethnicity in Catholic schools (Coleman & Hoffer, 1987; Coleman, Hoffer, & Kilgore, 1982; Polite, 1992, 2000).

Other evidence, however, indicates that Catholic schools do not always exhibit practices that reflect principles of social justice education. Most notably, these schools do not have strong track records of crafting effective service delivery models, particularly for students who present special needs (Weaver & Landers, 2000) and English language learners (Lawrence, 2000; O'Keefe & Murphy, 2000; Stevens-Arroyo & Pantoja, 2003). This book is an attempt to contribute to the growing recognition and amelioration of these weaknesses.

The field of Catholic education is increasingly articulating the premise that Catholic schools are compelled to instantiate Catholic social teaching by including and effectively serving traditionally marginalized students (Congregation for Catholic Education [CCE], 2007; Grace, 2002; O'Keefe, 1999; United States Conference of Catholic Bishops [USCCB], 2002, 2005a). This book seeks to support Catholic school leaders striving to do so. Fundamentally, the identity of Catholic schools strives toward universality. As Groome (1998) points out, the etymology of the term catholicity signifies welcoming everyone: "When such catholicity is the intent the particularity of Christianity can contribute most richly to the universal enterprise of education" (p. 12).

The central claim is that service delivery in Catholic schools needs to be approached in an inclusive manner. An inclusive approach to service delivery is one in which students are integrated into the heterogeneous school community, where students' needs are met in ways that keep them included, rather than in manners that exclude them (Frattura & Capper, 2007a). The values of Catholic social teaching, emphasizing human dignity, the common good, and a preferential option for the marginalized, direct Catholic schools to develop service delivery systems that welcome all students.

On the pages that follow, much attention is given to how Catholic schools can more effectively enact Catholic social teaching by designing their service delivery to reach traditionally marginalized students, particularly students with special needs and English language learners. This approach has three steps. First, a detailed description of the implications of Catholic social teaching for Catholic school educators is offered. Included in chapter 2 is an overview of Catholic social teaching as well as an analysis of key concepts within it. This lays the foundation for the book because it establishes that educating traditionally marginalized students is central to the mission of Catholic schools.

Second, service delivery to one type of traditionally marginalized students, those with special needs, is addressed. "Special needs" is an umbrella term encapsulating both diagnosed disabilities and undiagnosed barriers to student success. This service delivery is presented in broad strokes, including historical, legal, and resource dimensions across both public and private school sectors.

Catholic schools do not exist in a vacuum. They are influenced by the larger educational milieu. Many vital, pressing issues face Catholic schools, including improving professional development, redesigning curriculum, differentiating pedagogical strategies, budgeting efficiently, developing new resources, and building strong community relations. Most of these issues also face school leaders in other private sector schools, as well as schools in the public sector. Clearly, Catholic schools are distinct from public schools in numerous dimensions, such as their religious mission and identity, their financing and governance structures, and their recruitment and retention strategies.

Chapters 2 and 3 establish the foundation for presenting the model of inclusive service delivery for Catholic schools. In chapter 4, I present the established model of Integrated Comprehensive Services (Frattura & Capper, 2007a), weaving Catholic social teachings into the rationale and application of this model in a Catholic school context. I follow this in chapter 5 by extending the principles of Integrated Comprehensive Services to other dimensions of diversity.

In a sense, the text strives to answer the questions of why, what, and how. First, there is a focus on why Catholic school educators need to create inclusive service delivery systems; second, a focus on what inclusive service delivery systems are; third, a focus on how to move toward these inclusive service delivery systems in Catholic schools. Fundamentally, this is an effort to present a compelling case for how to bridge theory with practice. In the end, our successes and failures are measured not through abstract theory, but rather in specific actions in our daily work as educators. In terms of Catholic schools, the successes and failures come in our ability to match rhetoric with reality, and to sing the words "All are welcome" robustly, in a tune ringing true.

Catholic Social Teaching

Why do Catholic schools need to critically examine how they serve tradition-ally marginalized students? This is the fundamental question that needs to be resolved before school principals, teachers, board members and parents are going to invest precious time and resources toward this end. In a nutshell, the answer to the why question is simple: Catholic schools cannot claim to be truly Catholic if they do not diligently strive to adhere to the fundamental teachings of the Church, and Catholic social teaching unambiguously compels Catholic institutions to treat those on the margins with dignity.

Catholic social teaching (CST) forms a philosophical framework that the Church has developed since the late 19th century (Coleman, 1991; Vallely, 1998). In one sense CST applies broadly to messages on social matters spoken from a wide array of Catholic voices, ranging from Church officials to theologians to lay leaders. As the Pontifical Council for Justice and Peace (2004) describes, "The social doctrine belongs to the Church because the Church is the subject that formulates it, dissemi-nates it and teaches it....The whole of the Church community—priests, religious and laity—participates in the formulation of this social doctrine" (§79). In a more defined sense, CST typically references official messages on political, economic, and social issues conveyed by Church hierarchy, primarily through the offices of the Vatican and councils of bishops. CST represents the development of a coherent body of teachings regarding social relationships that developed over the past cen-tury (Coleman, 1991; Vallely, 1998). Hornsby-Smith (2006) points out that CST "is not static but dynamic in response to changing circumstances and needs" (p. 85). Finally, CST is directed by the Church to all people of good will, including Catho-lic followers, followers of other faith traditions, and followers of no faith tradition (Pontifical Council for Justice and Peace, 2004).

In this chapter we will examine how CST provides the foundational response to the question of why Catholic schools must create inclusive service delivery systems that meet the needs of those who have traditionally been marginalized. First we discuss CST in general. We then apply CST to Catholic schools. We conclude by suggesting that a focus on CST can catalyze Catholic schools to deliberately reform their structures and better serve students across multiple dimensions of diversity.

CST in General

The broader foundation of CST provides the principles upon which to craft an authentically Catholic approach to service delivery. A Catholic approach to service delivery strives to be inclusive toward all students not from an imposed legal obligation or utilitarian calculus, although a case can be made for each of these justifications. What drives the commitment to inclusivity in a Catholic approach to service delivery is an appreciation of the dignity of each individual person coupled with a commitment to the common good and a preferential option for those who tend to be marginalized. These tenets of CST in general provide a way of thinking about all students' needs that stands in contrast to a programmatic approach to service delivery.

In a sweeping overview of the social doctrine of the Church, the Pontifical Council for Justice and Peace (2004) explains the Church's deep commitment to promoting the social doctrine of CST:

> The way people live together in society often determines the quality of life and therefore the conditions in which every man and woman understand themselves and make decisions concerning themselves and their vocation. For this reason, the Church is not indifferent to what is decided, brought about or experienced in society; she is attentive to the moral quality—that is, the authentically human and humanizing aspects—of social life. Society—and with it, politics, the economy, labour, law, culture—is not simply a secular and worldly reality, and therefore outside or foreign to the message and economy of salvation....By means of her social doctrine, the Church takes on the task of proclaiming what the Lord has entrusted to her. She makes the message of the freedom and redemption wrought by Christ, the Gospel of the Kingdom, present in human history. (§§62-63)

The Council continues by promoting CST as integral to the mission of the Church to help people pursue the path of salvation: "This mission serves to give an overall shape to the Church's right and at the same time her duty to develop a social doctrine of her own and to influence society and societal structures with it by means of the responsibility and tasks to which it gives rise" (§69). In other words, promoting CST is a vital dimension of Catholic identity.

Foundational Anthropological Principles

CST is a form of moral theology seeking to affect people's motivations and consciences and societal norms (Pontifical Council for Justice and Peace, 2004, §73). As the Pontifical Council for Justice and Peace describes, "with her social doctrine the Church does not attempt to structure or organize society, but to appeal to, guide and form consciences" (§81). Over the decades CST has been grounded in both Scripture, which appeals to faith and revelation, and natural law theory, which provides a secular rationale (Curran, 2002; Hornsby-Smith, 2006). Natural law theory holds that human reason, infused by God's presence, can reliably guide all people in making moral judgments about what is right and what is wrong (Curran, 2002).

While scholars summarize CST in distinct ways (Byron, 1999; Dorr, 1992; Vallely, 1998), certain aspects are consistent throughout, including the foundational anthropological principles. A particular anthropology, or understanding of humanity, grounds CST. Curran (2002) explains that "without developing a systematic social ethics, Catholic social teaching recognizes the fundamental importance of anthropology as the basis for its teaching" (p. 127). Curran argues that two fundamental anthropological principles undergird CST: "The dignity or sacredness of the human person and the social nature of the person" (p. 131). These principles are grounded in the theology of Thomas Aquinas and the philosophy of Aristotle (Curran, 2002).

The recognition of the intrinsic dignity of the human person is a foundational principle upon which CST relies. *The Compendium of the Social Doctrine of the Church* (Pontifical Council for Justice and Peace, 2004) describes the human person as endowed with "an incomparable and inalienable dignity" (§105) and the central protagonist to all social life (§106). The pastoral constitution *On the Church in the Modern World*, or *Gaudium et Spes* (Vatican Council II, 1965a), teaches that people are endowed with intrinsic dignity, created in the image and likeness of God, and called "to communion with God...[and] invited to converse with God" (§19). People are "created by God's love and constantly preserved by it" (§19), and accordingly, "a special obligation binds us to make ourselves the neighbor of every person without exception" (§27). This understanding compels unambiguous social behavior:

> Respect and love ought to be extended also to those who think or act differently than we do in social, political and even religious matters. In fact, the more deeply we come to understand their ways of thinking through such courtesy and love, the more easily will we be able to enter into dialogue with them. (§28)

This principle of the dignity of the person implies that life is vocational. In the encyclical *Populorum Progressio*, Pope Paul VI (1967) argues that "every human life is called to some task by God" (§15) and that each individual is personally responsible for discerning his or her calling and developing his or her aptitudes and abilities. Additionally, this principle is grounded in what Curran (2002) describes as a "true, authentic, or transcendent humanism [which] recognizes the need for a basic level of material goods but warns against material goods becoming the be-all and end-all of human existence, smothering the more spiritual goods of authentic human development" (p. 131). Simply put, CST "develops from the principle that affirms the inviolable dignity of the human person" (Pontifical Council for Justice and Peace, 2004, §107).

Second is the anthropological principle that humans are social beings, living in relationships with one another and with all of creation. *Gaudium et Spes* (Vatican Council II, 1965a) articulates this principle by asserting that people cannot authentically live and develop our potential in isolation, but instead through relationships with others (§12) and that all of humanity is interrelated and called to treat one an-other as family (§24). This principle is captured in the notion of the common good, a central tenet of CST. In *Gaudium et Spes*, the common good is defined as "the sum of those conditions of social life which allow social groups and their individual members relatively thorough and ready access to their own fulfillment" (§26). In the encyclical *Populorum Progressio*, Pope Paul VI (1967) articulates how the principle of the common good compels people to be of service to one another:

> It is not just certain individuals but all...who are called to further the development of human society as a whole. Civilizations spring up, flourish and die. As the waves of the sea gradually creep farther and farther in along the shoreline, so the human race inches its way forward through history. We are the heirs of earlier generations, and we reap benefits from the efforts of our contemporaries; we are under obliga-tion to all....Therefore we cannot disregard the welfare of those who will come after us to increase the human family. The reality of human solidarity brings us not only benefits but also obligations. (§17)

In addition to these two foundational principles that human beings, by nature, are both dignified and social, Curran (2002) describes four other characteristics of Catholic anthropology embedded in CST. First, CST emphasizes the fulfillment of humans. "From a theological perspective," Curran argues, "the Catholic approach has insisted that the glory of God and human fulfillment are intimately related and not opposed to one another. The purpose of God in creating and redeeming human beings is the glory of God and human fulfillment" (p. 129). Second, this human fulfillment will not be complete in this world, where evil and suffering will remain a vexing dimension of reality. Third, both faith and works—belief and action—are critical components to living as a Catholic. Finally, "morality is intrinsic, not extrin-sic. Extrinsic morality regards the moral norm as something imposed on the human being from outside. Intrinsic morality regards morality as coming from within the human person and contributing to her or his fulfillment and happiness" (p. 130). In other words, the Catholic understanding is that God calls humans to certain duties because they are good and contribute to our fulfillment and happiness. "Something is commanded because it is good, not the other way around" (p. 130).

Core Foci of CST

These foundational anthropological principles provide the foci of CST. Coleman (1991) argues that through the 20th century CST has focused primarily on issues of family, work, and peace. Several biases have consistently emerged, including biases toward social rather than political revolution, toward a pluralist view of authority, and toward a balance of emphasis on social as well as individual rights.

No hard and fast rules dictate a discrete body of texts and tenets that comprise the official CST corpus. Pope Leo XIII's encyclical *Rerum Novarum*, published in 1891, is typically referenced as the first document articulating CST (Schuck, 1991).

As Curran (2002) states, this was a response to the "Enlightenment's emphasis on the individual, human freedom, and human reason totally cut off from any relationship to God and God's law" (p. 4), as well as changes in economics and demographics associated with the Industrial Revolution. More recently, Church documents from the Vatican, including documents of the Second Vatican Council and papal encyclicals, and documents from bishops form the foci of CST.

The foundational anthropological principles of CST, that humans have inherent dignity and are called to live in community and promote the common good, form the two most fundamental and ubiquitous values permeating these works. Other key themes that emerge tend to be directly related to these two principles. In terms congruent with the USCCB (2005b), the Archdiocese of St. Paul and Minneapolis, Office for Social Justice (2006) has produced a succinct and useful summary of 10 major themes of CST, outlined in Table 1.

The Compendium of the Social Doctrine of the Church (Pontifical Council for Justice and Peace, 2004) provides a rich overview of the official social doctrine that comprises CST. It identifies five core principles:

1. The Principle of the Common Good: All people have dignity, unity, and equality, and social conditions should affirm these for people both individually and collectively.
2. The Universal Destination of Goods: "God gave the earth to the whole human race for the sustenance of all its members, without excluding or favouring anyone" (§171).
3. The Principle of Subsidiarity: Decisions that can appropriately be made by more fundamental or basic social groups should not be made by more elevated or complex social groups (i.e., the government should not take away decisions that can be rightly made by the family).
4. Participation: People have a right and responsibility to participate in the cultural, economic, political, and social life of their community, seeking to serve the common good.
5. Solidarity: People are interdependent globally, and called to dismantle inequities that persist at systemic levels.

Additionally, the *Compendium* identifies four core social values that are inherent in the dignity of the human person and serve as reference points for enacting these principles. These values are truth, freedom, justice, and love.

Implication of CST

A core implication emerging through these foci is that CST compels Catholics, individually and institutionally, to behave in certain manners. An early and lucid articulation of this implication came from the Second Vatican Council. In forceful language, *Gaudium et Spes* (Vatican Council II, 1965a) explains that Christians, at once living on earth and looking toward eternal life in heaven, must balance faith with action:

Table 1 *Key Themes of Catholic Social Teaching*	
Theme	**Summary**
Dignity of the Human Person*	Human life is sacred, and the dignity of the human person is the starting point for a moral vision for society. The person is made in the image of God and is the reflection of God among us.
Common Good/ Community*	We realize our dignity and rights in relationship with others, in community. Human beings grow and achieve fulfillment in community. Human dignity is realized and protected in the context of relationships with the wider society.
Option for the Poor/ Vulnerable*	The moral test of a society is how it treats its most vulnerable members. The poor have the most urgent moral claim on the conscience of the nation. A healthy community is achieved when its members give special attention to those on the margins of society.
Rights and Responsibilities*	Each person has a right to life and what is needed for human decency—starting with food, shelter and clothing, employment, health care, and education. With these rights come responsibilities to each other, our families, and society.
Role of Government and Subsidiarity	The state has a positive moral function and is an instrument to promote human dignity, protect human rights, and build the common good. All people have a right and a responsibility to participate in political institutions. The principle of subsidiarity holds that the functions of government should be performed at the lowest level possible, as long as they can be performed adequately.
Economic Justice	All workers have a right to productive work, to decent and fair wages, to safe working conditions, and to organize and join unions. People have a right to economic initiative and private property, but these rights have limits. No one is allowed to amass excessive wealth when others lack the basic necessities of life.
Stewardship of God's Creation*	The goods of the earth are gifts from God, intended by God for the benefit of everyone. There is a "social mortgage" that guides our use of the world's goods, and we have a responsibility to care for these goods as stewards and trustees, not as mere consumers and users.
Promotion of Peace and Disarmament	Peace is a positive, action-oriented concept that involves mutual respect and confidence between peoples and nations. Peace is the fruit of justice and is dependent upon right order among human beings.
Participation	People have a right to participate in the economic, political, and cultural life of society. A fundamental demand of justice and a requirement for human dignity is that all people are assured a minimum level of participation in the community.
Global Solidarity and Development*	As one human family, our responsibilities to each other cross national, racial, economic, and ideological differences. Authentic development respects and promotes personal, social, economic, and political rights, including the rights of nations and of peoples, and avoids the extremists of underdevelopment on the one hand, and "superdevelopment" on the other.

Note. This list of key themes is adopted from the Office of Social Justice, Archdiocese of St. Paul and Minneapolis (2006). Themes identified with a "*" are directly reflected in the list of seven themes of Catholic social teaching from the United States Conference of Catholic Bishops (2005b).

This council exhorts Christians, as citizens of two cities, to strive to discharge their earthly duties conscientiously and in response to the Gospel spirit. They are mistaken who, knowing that we have here no abiding city but seek one that is to come, think that they may therefore shirk their earthly responsibilities. For they are forgetting that by the faith itself they are more obliged than ever to measure up to these duties, each according to his proper vocation. Nor, on the contrary, are they any less wide of the mark who think that religion consists in acts of worship alone and in the discharge of certain moral obligations, and who imagine they can plunge themselves into earthly affairs in such a way as to imply that these are altogether divorced from the religious life. This split between the faith which many profess and their daily lives deserves to be counted among the more serious errors of our age. (§43)

More recently, the Pontifical Council for Justice and Peace (2004) reaffirmed the importance of adhering to CST: "Insofar as it is part of the Church's moral teaching, the Church's social doctrine has the same dignity and authority as her moral teaching. It is authentic Magisterium, which obligates the faithful to adhere to it" (§80). Simply put, Catholics are not free to ignore CST, but instead are obligated to imbue their lives and actions and to interact in broader society in manners that reflect their identity as "witnesses to Christ" (Vatican Council II, 1965a, §43).

This core implication permeates the articulation of CST that has developed over the decades of the 20th century. It helps explain why CST emphasizes the structural, rather than merely the personal, dimension of injustice. In an extensive account of CST, Hornsby-Smith (2006) makes this point, distinguishing between ameliorating suffering (i.e., providing food to the hungry), and "seeking justice by addressing the causes of injustices and changing the structures which oppress" (p. 7). For example, in *Economic Justice for All*, the U.S. bishops (National Conference of Catholic Bishops [NCCB], 1986) employed CST to a critique of the economic order in the United States, asserting that the "dignity of the human person, realized in community with others, is the criterion against which all aspects of economic life must be measured" (p. 28).

Hornsby-Smith (2006) draws from the work of Holland and Henriot (1983) to outline a four-stage pastoral cycle of social action. First, we identify the needs that are salient in our social situation. Next, we analyze the causes of these needs. Third, we reflect on these analyses theologically, guided by both Scripture and Catholic social teaching. Finally, we structure our actions to remedy the unjust, sinful social structures. Hornsby-Smith points out that "the important point to note is that religiously inspired social action is cyclical and in a real sense unending. Each stage leads on to the next with the spiral deepening in its understanding and commitment." (p. 18). Hornsby-Smith continues:

Social analysis and theological reflection sharpen the awareness of the imperfections of the world in which we live and help us to transcend the boundaries of our own limited experiences and identify new issues. Social action alongside the poor or oppressed and a deeper awareness of their experiences challenge us to develop an interpretive social analysis on these and to reflect on them theologically in the light of scripture and the developments in Catholic social thought....Increasingly important, too, in this process is the place of prayer and spirituality as part of the scriptural and theological reflection and their consequent impact on the lifestyles and witness of actors. (p. 18)

Thus, the core implication of CST is that the beliefs of the faith must guide decisions and actions about social and organizational structures. We now turn to examine this implication of CST in the context of Catholic schools.

CST as Applied to Catholic Schools

Without question, CST applies to education. CST affirms that the family forms the original and fundamental role of educating the child (Pontifical Council for Justice and Peace, 2004). CST also holds schools in general, and Catholic schools in particular, as integral institutions in this role. As the Pontifical Council for Justice and Peace (2004) puts it, CST is "an expression of the Church's ministry of teaching" (§79).

Three central concepts from CST apply directly to the organization of Catholic schools: (a) human dignity, (b) the common good, and (c) a preferential option for the marginalized (Storz & Nestor, 2007). Two of these directly reflect the principles of anthropology described in the previous section. First, the Church considers each individual to be endowed with dignity that neither stems from a social contract nor is subject to a utilitarian calculus. Rather, it attributes the intrinsic value of the human person to their formation in the image and likeness of God (CCE, 2007; John Paul II, 1995; O'Collins, Kendall, & LaBelle, 2007). Second, human dignity is relational. As Hollenbach (1996) states, CST recognizes "that the dignity of human persons is achieved only in community with others" (p. 95). The common good is a balance between individual rights and the good of the wider society, and includes a "notion of integral human development...that no one should be excluded from the benefits of social development" (Vallely, 1998, p. 6). Vallely states,

> We contribute to the common good because we want to live in a society which is fair and just. If it is fair and just to others it will be fair and just to us too....The service of the common good is an end in itself. (p. 6)

The third value of CST extends beyond the notions of human dignity and the common good by placing a preferential option for those individuals who society marginalizes. This teaching holds that the Church is obligated to first serve, in the words of the World Synod of Catholic Bishops (1971), "those who suffer violence and are oppressed by unjust systems and structures" (p. 5). This dimension critiques institutions, policies, and practices that allow or exacerbate poverty, inequality, and injustice. Dorr (1992) finds this dimension the seminal, connecting issue tying together a century of different Church leaders responding to situations around the world. Dorr describes the Church's "option for the poor" as "special care or preference for people or groups who are marginalized in human society" (p. 7).

Applying CST to Catholic Schooling: Curricular Versus Structural Reform

Under the broader umbrella of CST, these three particular values—human dignity, the common good, and a preferential option for the marginalized—apply most directly to Catholic schools. Generally, educators either emphasize curricular or structural applications.

In many ways, especially in the United States, Church teachings have emphasized curricular applications of CST. These curricular applications also extend to all CST themes. For instance, lessons in social studies might weave in ideas about rights and responsibilities or on the role of government and subsidiarity, or biology lessons might incorporate the CST notion of stewardship. Certainly the religious curriculum in Catholic schools should address CST, which is woven throughout the Catechism of the Catholic Church (Holy See, 2000).

This curricular emphasis is frequently reflected in publications and conferences as well. For instance, exemplars of integrating and applying the themes and values of CST into service projects, courses, and ceremonies can be found in articles in *Momentum*, the journal of the National Catholic Educational Association (NCEA), as well as at NCEA conference sessions.

In the wake of Vatican II, the United States bishops published a series of documents that addressed CST (NCCB, 1972, 1989, 1993, 1995, 1998a, 1998b). With the exception of an occasional reference to education, these documents largely avoid applying CST to structurally reforming Catholic schools. The bishops established a Task Force on Catholic Social Teaching and Catholic Education in 1995 and published a summary report 3 years later, yet the tenor of the report emphasized the teaching of CST in Catholic schools and educational programs, not integrating CST into the structures of the schools themselves. The bishops acknowledge that education is one of the Church's most important forums for sharing and demonstrating commitment to human dignity and social justice, but in ways emphasize communicating this message over implementing it.

In contrast to these curricular applications, I emphasize applying CST as a guide to structural reform. From this perspective, CST directs Catholic school leaders to ask specific questions about how they apply the values of CST in policies and practices within their schools. For instance, school administrators ask: "How does our delivery of instruction balance the values of human dignity with the common good?" School board members determine, "How does our financial planning create a preferential option for the marginalized?"

The emphasis on CST as a guide for structural reform directs attention to a core struggle for Catholic schools in the last 4 decades. Carr (1997) argues that "one of [the Catholic Church's] greatest challenges is integrating more fully [its] social justice heritage into [its] educational programs" (p. 7). The field of Catholic education has unambiguously held that CST compels Catholic schools to strive to include traditionally marginalized students, yet practices of exclusion and elitism in recruitment and retention of students by Catholic schools persist.

Applying CST to structural over curricular reform is supported by teachings of the Church, stemming back to Vatican II. *The Declaration on Christian Education* (Vatican Council II, 1965b) directs several applications of CST to schools. The declaration clarifies that it is appropriate for religious schools to pursue cultural goals and the natural development of the child in a manner not unlike the public schools, but that the religious school is distinctive in its conception of community (Convey, 1992). They are distinctive from public schools in their attempt to "generate a community climate in the school that is permeated by the Gospel spirit of freedom and love...[and to] relate all human culture to the Gospel" (Vatican Council II, 1965b, §8). The document continues by entreating members of the Catholic community "to spare no sacrifice in helping Catholic schools...especially in caring for the needs of those who are poor in the goods of this world or who are deprived of the assistance and affection of a family or who are strangers to the gift of Faith" (§9). As Hamilton (2008a) describes, one of the core effects of Vatican II on U.S. Catholic schools was that "it established social justice as a key goal for the Church, giving its leaders a renewed mission to help poor and minority students, regardless of their faith" (p. 13).

This theme continued in subsequent publications from the Vatican. A decade after Vatican II the publication of *The Catholic School* (CCE, 1977), continued to connect CST directly to Catholic school structures. Here, a preferential option for the marginalized was spelled out directly: "First and foremost the Church offers its educational service to the poor" (§58). Catholic schooling, it continues, should not "exclusively or predominantly... [serve] wealthier social classes...[lest it] favour a society which is unjust" (§58). Most recently, in *Educating Together in Catholic Schools* (CCE, 2007), the Church teaches that by welcoming all dimensions of diversity of the human family, "the educational community of the Catholic school aims at creating increasingly deeper relationships of communion that are in themselves educational" (§37). The emphasis here is that the actions of the teachers and the composition of the student body, by embracing this diversity, provide a "witness of communion":

> By giving witness of communion, the Catholic educational community is able to educate for communion, which...animates the project of formation for living together in harmony and being welcoming. Not only does it cultivate in the students the cultural values that derive from the Christian vision of reality, but it also involves each one of them in the life of the community, where values are mediated by authentic interpersonal relationships among the various members that form it, and by the individual and community acceptance of them. In this way, the life of communion of the educational community assumes the value of an educational principle, of a paradigm that directs its formational action as a service for the achievement of a culture of communion. (§39)

Applying CST to Structural Reform Across Multiple Dimensions of Diversity
These two divergent applications of CST—one emphasizing the integration of the themes and values of CST into the teaching and learning curriculum, and the other using CST to guide structural reform of the teaching and learning environment— are neither incompatible nor mutually exclusive. However, the latter is more difficult to implement than the former. Simply put, teaching about a preferential option for the marginalized is easier than reforming patterns of recruitment and retention of students to apply a preferential option for students with special needs. Integrating lessons about immigrant communities can be accomplished more readily than improving outreach efforts welcoming these students into schools.

When Catholic educators do seek to apply CST to structurally reform Catholic schools, their efforts tend not to extend across multiple dimensions of diversity, but instead to focus on improving services for students in poverty. Echoing the language in *The Catholic School* (CCE, 1977), Dorr (1992) applies CST to critique Catholic schools that serve the wealthy, asserting that such schools reinforce unjust social orders prioritizing the interests of the rich and powerful.

O'Keefe also applies CST to critique structures of Catholic schools which marginalize students in poverty. Discussing the Church's social teaching of a preference for the poor, O'Keefe (1996) notes that the "implication for Catholic schools is obvious. If segments of the population are marginalized, the Church is obliged to make extraordinary efforts to rectify social fragmentation" (pp. 190-191). O'Keefe goes on to assert that the schools should also be anti-racist, noting that the "Church eschews a model of assimilation to European cultural patterns and adopts a philosophy of cultural pluralism" (p. 192). O'Keefe (2000) also finds that "because of its gospel mission, the Catholic community is irrevocably committed to those in greatest need" (p. 227), and argues that this commitment applies directly to Catholic schools in urban settings.

Hamilton (2008a) draws direct connections between Vatican II and the increased trends in Catholic schools to serve students that were both more religiously heterogeneous and of lower socioeconomic status:

> Vatican II's emphasis on social justice came in the midst of America's civil rights movement, Lyndon Johnson's War on Poverty, and the advent of Title I aid to high-poverty schools under the federal Elementary and Secondary Education Act. It was also around this time that parochial school enrollments began to drop as successful Catholic families moved out of the urban areas where most Catholic schools were located and into burgeoning suburbs where nearly everyone attended public schools. The Church responded quickly and generously by keeping many of its inner-city schools open—despite the changing demographics—to serve poor, non-Catholic schools. Given their track record of serving poor Catholic families, such schools were well positioned to teach academics and character to poor non-Catholics. (p. 13)

While the structural application of CST has tended to focus on issues of poverty, this is starting to extend to other dimensions of diversity. Martin and Litton (2004) take a particularly expansive view, encouraging Catholic schools to promote equity for students across multiple dimensions of diversity, including sexual orientation and religion. McLaughlin (2000) draws upon a 1998 publication by the CCE to argue that principles of "solidarity with the oppressed, distributive justice, preferential option for the poor, democracy, power sharing, and basic human rights" (p. 283) should govern the formation of community within Catholic schools. Barton (2000) articulates a vision of Catholic schooling that is intrinsically inclusive of all students, including those with special needs.

To recap, CST articulates general guidance for Catholics on applying their faith to actions in society. In the context of Catholic schools, the themes and values of CST can be applied in specific ways to both curricular matters and structural reforms. Evidence suggests that CST is increasingly seen as a guide to structurally reform Catholic schools to improve service delivery across multiple dimensions of diversity. The final section of this chapter describes this as a paradigm shift for Catholic school communities that fundamentally depends on school leadership.

Breaking the Grammar of Catholic Schooling

Grammar signifies the underlying rules that organize a language. Tyack and Tobin (1994) coined the phrase the "grammar of schooling" to explain the structures and rules that organize education in an underlying, unquestioned manner. As I have argued elsewhere, "in an analogous manner, a grammar of Catholic schooling has inhibited the incorporation of the values of CST into the structure of schools" (Scanlan, 2008b, p. 30). Catholic schools effectively employ CST as a guide to structural reform only when leaders in the school community confront this grammar.

The grammar of Catholic schooling has allowed schools to ignore or justify the incongruity between values of CST and structures of exclusion. Put another way, Catholic educators have frequently failed to conceptualize how their schools can be structured to implement CST because such structures fall outside the underlying organizational principles of the schools. An example illustrating how this grammar operates and how it can be confronted can be seen in the service of students in poverty. Funding schemes based on tuition and parish subsidy form a fundamental organizational principle for most Catholic elementary schools. Such funding schemes preclude extensive access to students in poverty. Exceptions, such as scholarships, are certainly made. By definition, however, these are exceptions to the rule. The basic assumptions of the funding scheme create the grammar in which the schools operate, and this grammar does not allow for the school to enroll significant numbers of students in poverty. This grammar can be broken by school leaders who reformulate the funding schemes, such as through publically funded vouchers, school choice efforts, tuition tax credits, or through stewardship models of community support (Hamilton, 2008b).

I argue that Catholic schools can effectively apply CST as a guide to structural reform only when leaders in these communities recognize and address the barriers imposed by the grammar of Catholic schooling. Underlying assumptions in the school tend to make the education of traditionally marginalized students the exception, while the values of human dignity, the common good, and a preferential option for the marginalized direct schools to make these the norm. Confronting this grammar allows schools to envision and articulate a service delivery system that embraces students across multiple dimensions of diversity, from those in poverty to English language learners, addressing racial, ethnic, and cultural dimensions as well as exceptionalities.

Catholic school leaders, specifically bishops, principals, presidents, superintendents, and board members, are invariably the impetus behind school communities that attempt to break the grammar of Catholic schooling. Leaders are at the core of effective and sustainable Catholic school communities (Convey, 2008; Hamilton, 2008b; Hunt, Oldenski, & Wallace, 2000; Schuttloffel, 2003). As Convey (2008) states, "When good leadership is in place, schools thrive. Problematic leadership has drastic consequences—some immediate, some delayed" (p. 28). Recent empirical literature makes clear that Catholic schools that pursue policies and practices reflective of CST depend upon strong leadership, especially at the building level (O'Keefe, 1999, 2000; Schuttloffel, 2003).

The principal plays the central role in operationalizing what might otherwise remain abstract value propositions. According to Bryk and colleagues (1993), Catholic schools emphasize the spiritual and moral dimensions of the individual, the dignity of the human person, community, social justice, and the common good. These characteristics are strikingly similar to the basic tenets of CST (e.g., human dignity, the common good, and a preferential option for the marginalized). Bryk et al. found these integrated into the school culture through incorporating values of Christian personalism and subsidiarity. Christian personalism "signifies a moral conception of social behaviour in a just community" (p. 301). The value of subsidiarity enabled this personalism to take hold:

> Subsidiarity means that the schools reject a purely bureaucratic conception of an organization....Decentralization of school governance is not chosen purely because it is more efficient...rather decentralization is predicated in the view that personal dignity and human respect are advanced when work is organized in small communities where dialogue and collegiality may flourish. (pp. 301-302)

The key to translating this ideology into the culture was the principal (Bryk et al., 1993). These leaders employed language imbued with spirituality when describing their schools and their actions to achieve goals. This allowed them to underpin policies and procedures with the fundamental missions and values of the school. It is "the underlying values of the institution—shared by its members—[which provides] the animating force for the entire enterprise" (p. 279).

In a study of parochial school administrators in Britain, Grace (1996) found similar trends of leaders influencing culture. Describing the mission of the school in terms of Gospel (i.e., biblical) values, the teachings of Christ, and the nurturance of community, the administrators Grace interviewed engaged in what he called a discourse of mission:

> The realization of this mission was...dependent upon their own leadership quali-
> ties; support from parents...and the parish; the commitments of teachers, not all
> of whom were Catholics; the response of pupils, many from nominally Catholic
> homes and an increasing proportion from non-Catholic backgrounds. (p. 74)

O'Keefe (1999) characterizes the contemporary Catholic school in consistent terms. The characteristics involve religious identity, strong tradition and ritual, values of subsidiarity, community, and ecumenism, critiques of structural sin, and teleological nature. These characteristics, O'Keefe concludes, in the hands of visionary leadership from the entire Catholic community, will allow the schools to contribute to the common good. The framework for developing Catholic school leaders that Cook and Durow (2008) formulate reflects aspects of CST, including the personal attributes of a commitment to social justice. Elsewhere I have argued that leadership in Catholic schools is central to engaging caregivers (Scanlan, 2008a) and enacting CST (Scanlan, 2006a, 2006b, 2008b).

In conclusion, there is widespread agreement that CST directs Catholic schools to open their doors to all children, especially those marginalized (Barton, 2000; Benton & Owen, 1995, 1997; Long & Schuttloffel, 2006; Owen, 1988, 1997, 2002). The three core values of CST—human dignity, the common good, and a preferential option for the marginalized—compel Catholic school educators in general, and school leaders in particular to structure their schools in certain ways. The policies and practices in the school should serve traditionally marginalized students (Storz & Nestor, 2007). Specifically, the emphases of CST on human dignity, the common good, and a preferential option for the marginalized obligate these leaders to enact service delivery models demonstrating inclusivity toward traditionally marginalized students.

In a manner of speaking, this chapter answers the foundational question: Why do Catholic school educators need to critically examine the ways that our schools serve traditionally marginalized students? We need to do so because CST compels us to serve human dignity and the common good, always placing the marginalized at the center of our focus. This question of why brings me to recall my first years of teaching at St. Gabriel School, in the early 1990s, where the music teacher led the students in the Kirk Franklin song, "Why We Sing" (Warren, 1997, pp. 347-349). The song opens with the lines, "Someone asked the question, why do we sing? When we lift our hands to Jesus, what do we really mean?" Part of the answer comes a few lines later: "I sing because I'm happy. I sing because I'm free. His eye is on the sparrow, and that's the reason why I sing." The eye of God on the sparrow, a reference to the passage from the Gospel of Matthew describing God as attending to all forms of life (Matthew 10:29-31), was first captured in lyrics a century ago (C. D. Martin, 1905). God's love for all life, stretching to the smallest, most vulnerable forms, is the reason why we, too, strive to welcome all into our Catholic schools, and place a special emphasis on those who are vulnerable.

From this question of why we now turn to consider questions of what and how. Specifically, what service delivery models are in place for students with special needs, and how can we follow CST to transform these models?

Service Delivery to
Traditionally Marginalized Students

If Catholic social teaching (CST) compels Catholic schools to serve traditionally marginalized students, what does this look like? Clearly, simply admitting these students to school does not suffice; we need specific strategies to educate them. In this chapter, we turn to address these matters by taking a broad look at systems of service delivery, and a focused look at this for students with special needs.

Service delivery refers to how different groupings of students access educational services. As schools strive to meet the different needs that students exhibit, they develop different services to delivery. Support for students in poverty, for instance, is typically funded from Title I dollars and has historically been delivered by a designated teacher to students who qualify because their families are of low socioeconomic status. Bilingual, gifted and talented, and special education are some of the primary examples of other types of services. Generally speaking, public schools do not integrate these services into a comprehensive, coherent approach. Instead, they are fragmented and disjointed. This is largely due to the history of programmatic service delivery, which has resulted in a large number of discrete programs serving specific populations (Capper, et al., 2000; Frattura & Capper, 2007a).

Catholic schools, however, find themselves in a different situation. While many traditionally marginalized students have found Catholic schools to be effective educational institutions, these schools have seldom developed specific systems of service delivery for traditionally marginalized students. For instance, most Catholic schools have undeveloped or underdeveloped systems to deliver services to students with special needs or students who are English language learners.

As we will see, this actually poses an advantage for Catholic schools striving to develop inclusive service delivery systems. Public schools find themselves struggling to transform programmatic approaches to service delivery, which tend to be inefficient and ineffective. Shedding the old and starting the new entails overcoming barriers of inertia; people who are invested in the current approach resist change. Catholic schools, on the other hand, lacking an existing system, may be more open to any approach to service delivery, especially regarding students with special needs and English language learners. Starting from scratch can be easier than retrofitting and redesigning an existing model.

We begin this chapter by placing systems of service delivery in the context of the historical pursuit of educational equity. Making progress in providing educational equity requires developing effective strategies of schooling for traditionally marginalized students. This context lays the foundation for examining service delivery for students with special needs, which comprises the second part of this chapter. In a subsequent chapter we will address how these same principles apply to service delivery for English language learners.

Social Justice Education: The Pursuit of Educational Equity

Catholic schools do not exist in a vacuum, but instead are situated in the broader field of education. Within this field, a central issue that has emerged over the course of the 20th century is social justice education. Social justice education involves the pursuit of equitable education for all students. What has this pursuit achieved? An optimistic perspective would cast this journey as a movement transforming segregatory service delivery structures to inclusive ones. Lipsky and Gartner (1996) describe the educational experiences of traditionally marginalized groups as evolving through three stages. First, students were formally, legally excluded. Next, they were formally included by judicial or legislative requirements, but still functionally excluded in many ways. The third stage is one of progress toward policies and practices of functional inclusion.

Arguably, these historical stages have applied to students across multiple dimensions of diversity, including race and ethnicity, socioeconomic status, linguistic heritage, and exceptionality. Students of color, for instance, were historically excluded from public schooling in the United States. Even after the abolition of slavery, African Americans were formally segregated for half a century, from *Plessy v. Ferguson* in 1896 until *Brown v. Board of Education* in 1954. The second stage toward formal inclusion came in *Brown* when the Supreme Court officially ruled that separate schooling for people of color was inherently unequal. This victory against de jure segregation gave way to a protracted battle against de facto segregation, on which no significant progress was made for over a decade (Chemerinsky, 2005; Orfield, 2001). This second stage shifted toward the third in 1964. That year the Supreme Court ruling in *Griffin v. County School Board* alongside the passage of Title VI of the Civil Rights Act both spurred more concrete movement of public sector schools toward desegregation.

In the 1960s-1970s progress ensued toward improved educational equity across other dimensions of diversity as well. For instance, Title 1 of the Elementary and Secondary Education Act of 1965 provided compensatory funding to schools serving students in poverty. The Equal Educational Opportunities Act of 1974 spelled out the obligation of public schools toward language-minority students:

> No state shall deny equal educational opportunity to an individual on account of his or her race, color, sex, or national origin, by…the failure of an educational agency to take appropriate action to overcome language barriers that impede equal participation by its students in its instructional programs. (20 U.S.C. §1703)

Finally, in 1975, Public Law 94-142, the Education for All Handicapped Children Act (which was later transformed into the Individuals with Disabilities Education Act, or IDEA) required that students with disabilities were provided free, appropriate public education in the least restrictive environment.

Despite these sequential gains, the path toward educational equity has hardly been a steady march from exclusion to inclusion. In their recent analysis of racial transformation and resegregation patterns in schools, Orfield and Lee (2007) describe the complexity of this journey in terms of race:

> Any serious student of the history of American race relations knows that racial progress has not been a straight path and that the burst of massive change associated with the Civil War and Reconstruction and the civil rights era of the 1960s are the great exceptions to long periods of stasis and regression in civil rights policy. (p. 13)

In point of fact, despite significant legislative gains, social justice education has remained an elusive goal. Massive gaps persist in the educational attainment by students across multiple dimensions of diversity (Bedsworth, Colby, & Doctor, 2006; The Education Trust, 2006). There are many reasons for these gaps, including the significant social and economic inequities in which schools operate (Kantor & Lowe, 2006). The pursuit of educational equity for traditionally marginalized students across most dimensions of diversity continues to be a complex and contentious journey.

Catholic Schools and Educational Equity

Catholic schools have played a paradoxical role in this pursuit. On one hand, they have provided a model of schooling that seems to promote educational equity. On the other hand, the schools exhibiting this are declining at alarming rates. Catholic schools, from their inception through the 1960s, were almost exclusively Catholic, especially at the elementary level (Buetow, 1988). Among this religious homogeneity, however, there was considerable diversity across other dimensions. The schools included many Catholics who can be characterized as traditionally marginalized—poor students, immigrants, English language learners, and minorities (Baker, 1999; Jacobs, 1998a).

Jacobs (1998a) explains that religious communities often financed schools in creative ways in order "to provide Catholic education in many locales, especially for poor and marginalized youth" (p. 369). Jacobs uses the situation of one religious order as an example:

> For the Ursulines, the funding formula was straightforward: the Sisters charged tuition to educate children of the wealthy upper—and merchant—class. These tuition revenues made it possible not only to provide for the religious community's sustenance but also to fund other sisters to engage in teaching children of economically

disadvantaged working class and poor parents, based on their ability to pay or free of charge. (p. 369)

Jacobs (1998a) explains this decision as rooted in a principle of Catholic social teaching, distributive justice: "Members of the community who possess more abundant resources bear a concomitant obligation to share their excess with others who do not share as abundantly in needed resources" (p. 369). Along with students from low socioeconomic status, these schools served significant numbers of immigrants and ethnic minorities, due to the fact that many Catholics were from these populations (Buetow, 1988; Morris, 1997).

Strong evidence suggests that Catholic schools have not only served traditionally marginalized students, but have been effective institutions at promoting educational equity for these students (Baker, 1999; Bryk et al., 1993; Cattaro, 2002; Coleman et al., 1982; Davis, 1990; Fenzel & Monteith, 2008; Jacobs, 1998a, 1998b, 1998c; O'Keefe et al., 2004; Owens, 2005; Polite, 1992, 2000; Sanders, 1977; Walch, 1996). Much of this work builds from the original finding that Coleman and colleagues asserted in 1982, that Catholic schools were more integrated and produced stronger student outcomes than their public school counterparts. Subsequent literature examined how specific Catholic parishes have cultivated school communities' welcoming toward students of color and students in poverty (e.g., Fenzel & Monteith, 2008). The seminal work of Bryk and colleagues (1993) describes several reasons for the success of Catholic schools in promoting educational equity, including: holding all students to common academic goals, fostering communal organizations with supportive structures and shared value systems, cultivating a common school philosophy grounded in social justice values and strong personal relationships, and operating with decentralized governance structure and local autonomy.

While Catholic schools promote educational equity by effectively educating traditionally marginalized students, they also increasingly exclude these very students from their schools (Baker & Riordan, 1998; Hamilton, 2008b). Currently, Catholic schools that are most vulnerable to face barriers to viability are the ones that are also most aligned to Catholic social teaching by serving significant numbers of traditionally marginalized students (Bryk, 2009). A factor related to this is the failure of Catholic schools to develop equitable service delivery for traditionally marginalized students. We now turn to examine this service delivery for students with special needs.

Service Delivery Models for Students with Special Needs

Across public and private education sectors, service delivery models for students with special needs have progressed from formal exclusion to espoused inclusion to practiced inclusion. Winzer (1993) titles the history of special education as a movement "from isolation to integration." Historically "disability" has a pejorative connotation, and people of color, immigrants, and women have been disparaged as "disabled" (Winzer, 1993). As Baynton (2001) points out, the typical response of distancing one's own group from imputations of disability, is a strategy which "tacitly accept[ed] the idea that disability is a legitimate reason for inequality" (p. 51), contributing to the persistence of prejudice against people with disabilities.

Service delivery models to students with special needs have reflected these prejudices. Kugelmass (2004) recounts that special education service delivery in public schools was "built on instructional models that were designed to remedy deficits" (p. 8). Services come as a result of students' failure "to successfully negotiate the mandated curriculum. If their failure is determined to be the result of a specific set of factors defined as a disability, they become classified as eligible for special education" (p. 8). While providing opportunities to students who would have otherwise been underserved or excluded from schools, they reflect "the belief that failure in school is the result of problems within the child…[leaving] the relationship between context, culture, social interaction, and learning…largely ignored" (p. 8). Kugelmass credits critical analysis by constituents of these deficit models of service delivery, particularly in the past 2 decades, with leading to increased "integration of culturally and individually appropriate instruction with constructivist practices" (p. 10) resulting in inclusive service delivery.

Carrington and Elkins (2002) summarize inclusive service delivery in the following way:

> Inclusive education signifies much more than the presence of students with disabilities in regular classrooms. It has developed from a long history of educational innovation and represents school improvement on many levels for all students….It is about celebrating difference in dignified ways….Above all, it is about a philosophy of acceptance where all people are valued and treated with respect. (p. 51)

In the final decades of the 20th century federal legislation and regulation emerged promoting inclusive service delivery. First, Section 504 of the Rehabilitation Act of 1973 provides protection from discrimination against individuals with disabilities. Protections of Section 504 apply to individuals who have—or are regarded as having—a physical or mental impairment that substantially limits their major life activities. If such individuals are otherwise qualified to participate in school programs or activities, they must be allowed to continue to do so with this impairment as long as this can be reasonably accommodated. Reasonable accommodations may include minor adjustments to policies and procedures (Russo, Massucci, Osborne, & Cattaro, 2002). Significantly for Catholic schools, Section 504 applies to schools in both the public and private sector that receive federal aid (Scanlan, in press-b).

Second, the Education for All Handicapped Children Act (P.L. 94-142) was introduced in 1975 and subsequently reauthorized as the Individuals with Disabilities Education Act (IDEA) in 1990, 1997, and 2004. While Section 504 requires schools to respond with reasonable accommodations once they are made aware of disabilities, under IDEA "public school districts must actively seek out school-age persons in need of related and support services and then act affirmatively to provide those services necessary for students to participate in education" (Mawdsley, 2000, p. 244). This law sought "to provide access to equal education opportunity for children with disabilities who had systematically been excluded from the nation's public schools" (Prasse, 2006, p. 8).

Significantly, IDEA applies to students in public school settings differently than those in private schools. IDEA compels public schools to provide students with disabilities a "free, appropriate public education" (FAPE) in the "least restrictive environment" (LRE). By contrast, IDEA does not apply to private schools in nearly the same manner. Private schools are not obliged to provide FAPE in the LRE, and when parents place their children in private schools they forfeit these rights protected under IDEA (Russo et al., 2002). The reauthorization of IDEA in 2004 clarified that children with diagnosed disabilities who are parentally placed in private schools have, as a group, a right to a proportionate share of IDEA funds. This does not necessarily translate into provision of services to an individual child with a disability whose parents chose to enroll him or her in a specific Catholic school. Such a child is grouped with all other children in the district who also happen to be diagnosed with disabilities and attending private schools. Private school officials must consult with their public school colleagues negotiating how the funds allocated for this pool of students will be spent (McDonald, 2005, 2007a, 2007b).

Within the public school context, IDEA directs special education service delivery to be approached in a certain manner. Without directly referencing inclusivity, IDEA implies that students by default be included in the regular education classrooms, and schools proposing to remove a child from the regular education classroom must prove that partial or total removal is required (National Council on Disability, 2000; TASH, 2000). The National Council on Disability describes this clearly: "Every step away from the regular classroom must be accompanied by a compelling educational rationale, in light of the law's preference for educating children with disabilities in the regular classroom alongside their nondisabled peers." Additionally, IDEA emphasizes that it is not enough for "students with disabilities to be present in a general education classroom; they must be provided with the supports and supplementary aides necessary to enhance their participation and progress in the curriculum" (Pugach & Warger, 2001, p. 194).

Under IDEA each student has a right to be assessed, and, if diagnosed with a disability, to receive individualized planning and programming in the form of an individualized education program (IEP). This right extends to students in public and private schools. The provision of the IEP, however, is only guaranteed in the public school. In other words, any child can be tested if a disability is suspected. If a disability is diagnosed, any child can receive the IEP laying out how the disability would be accommodated in the public school setting. The private schools may choose to implement such accommodations, but are not obliged to do so.

In determining appropriate service delivery that is in accord with an IEP, courts have consistently compelled school districts to base their decisions on the individual needs of each child, considering both the academic and non-academic benefits of placing a child in an inclusive setting as well as the effects the child would have on others in this setting and the cost of various service delivery options (Stout, 2001). As Mawdsley (2000) explains, "the assumption under IDEA is that FAPE will require that children with disabilities be placed with those who are nondisabled" (p. 245). Mawdsley also notes that IDEA redefines how schools and families interact regarding service delivery because "parents of students with disabilities and in need of special education services are treated as equals in the determination of [IEP] services" (p. 244).

Persisting Programmatic Approaches

These legal developments of Section 504 and IDEA have promoted shifts from programmatic approaches to service delivery for students with special needs toward inclusionary ones. While current literature on service delivery models for students with disabilities articulates strong rationales for meeting the needs of all students in integrated, differentiated, heterogeneous settings (National Council on Disability, 2000; Turnbull, Turnbull, Shank, & Smith, 2003), and the legislative pressures promote this, the reality of most students' experiences is less ideal. Despite the preference in federal laws of IDEA and Section 504 for inclusive service delivery, public schools have inconsistently educated students with disabilities alongside those who do not have disabilities (U.S. Department of Education, 2003). Students with disabilities continue to be largely educated away from general education classrooms, with 27% spending part (21-60%) and 17% spending most (> 60%) of their school day in segregated settings (Artiles, Trent, & Palmer, 2004). Due to the persistent overrepresentation of people of color in special education (Ferri & Connor, 2005; Valenzuela, Copeland, Qi, & Park, 2006), segregatory service delivery models contribute to increased racial segregation in schools (Reid & Valle, 2004; Spring, 1989; Ware, 2002).

Segregatory service delivery within special education is an outgrowth of the historical trend of schools placing the blame on students and families that they struggle to serve (Taylor, 1988, 2001; Winzer, 1993). Taylor (2001) critiques the notion of a "least restrictive environment" as not only imprecise and subjective, but inherently flawed by suggesting that people with disabilities fall on a continuum between receiving intensive services in segregated settings and receiving less intensive services in integrated settings. As Taylor (2001) points out, "segregation and integration, on the one hand, and intensity of services, on the other, are separate dimensions. Any health-related, educational, or habilitative service that can theoretically be provided in a segregated setting can be provided in an integrated setting" (p. 19).

Segregatory special education policies and practices, Ware (2004) explains, are connected to schools' penchant for blaming "the disabled student for their own failure to measure up to an arbitrary standard for normalcy and…[focusing on] student pathology rather than organizational pathology" (p. 154). Reid and Valle's (2004) critical analysis of instructional practices to students with learning disabilities (LD) captures the insidious effects of such service delivery models on students:

> In response to the occasion of a child's failure to learn, a cadre of professionals who together constitute the LD service industry stand poised to apply their scientific tools to the task of identifying the educational needs of the individual child. Once the child is characterized as having "special needs," the scientific, medical, and psychological discourses reposition the child who fails to learn as the child who *requires* an education that is, by definition, special—so special that it may mean an education apart from children without a "special" designation. (p. 471)

Reid and Valle advocate for reconceptualizing LD as a manifestation of "human variation rather than pathology" (p. 473) and argue that "when we view variation as productive and natural, we can address it through the differentiation of instruction, not through the sorting of children into already available categories—a very different way of thinking about both disability and classrooms" (p. 473).

While evidence suggests that inclusive service delivery is at times preferable to some teachers (Kugelmass, 2004; Sindelar, Shearer, Yendol-Hoppey, & Liebert, 2006), research shows such practices are difficult to establish and maintain (Brownell, Adams, Sindelar, Waldron, & Vanhover, 2006). Both special educators and general education classroom teachers have historically defended the exclusion of some children from general education programs for multiple reasons, including suspicion of top-down directives and lack of preparation (Kugelmass). Sindelar et al. argue that "inclusion is often misunderstood and sometimes resisted by teachers, and it is not always fully understood or supported by school administrators" (p. 319). Their longitudinal qualitative study showed a school moving from inclusive to pullout service delivery due to "changes in leadership, teacher turnover, and a shift in district and state priorities" (p. 325). In addition, some general education teachers struggle to engage in collaboration with special education peers to enact inclusive service delivery. Teachers with a strong knowledge base in curriculum and pedagogy as well as dispositions toward adaptive pedagogical strategies, are strong candidates for developing collaborative relationships. Those with less developed knowledge bases and more rigid, teacher-centered beliefs about managing student behavior are less able to do so.

In sum, few schools, let alone systems of schools, provide service delivery that is comprehensively inclusive. Instead, programmatic approaches to student struggles are the norm. Students who have diagnosed disabilities receive pull-out support from the special education teacher. Students in poverty receive pull-out support from the Title I teacher. Students who are English language learners are clustered together to work with the bilingual teacher. Students who are identified as gifted are pulled out to work with another teacher on accelerated work in a gifted and talented program. And the students without any of these labels or identifications are the ones left in the regular classroom.

Best Practices in Special Education Service Delivery

Though programmatic approaches to special education service delivery persist, progress toward inclusive service delivery is gaining momentum. In 2002, a Presidential Commission concluded that the system of special education was in need of significant reform, and recommended that such reform should emphasize (a) providing opportunities and achieving outcomes for students, (b) preventing student failure, and (c) fostering collaboration among general and special educators in the efforts to educate all children together (President's Commission on Excellence in Special Education, 2002).

The current best practices in special education service delivery are described as "Responses to Intervention" (RTI; Hale, Kaufman, Naglieri, & Kavale, 2006; Martinez, Nellis, & Prendergast, 2006; National Association of State Directors of Special Education [NASDSE], 2006). Three core dimensions comprise RTI. The first is the importance of providing high quality instruction and interventions to all students (NASDSE, 2006). This emphasizes that the role of a service delivery model is to look at the teaching and learning environment for all students. It aligns with the first and third dimensions of the Presidential Commission's recommendations. Schools must focus on providing opportunities and achieving outcomes for all students, through the collaborative efforts of all the educators sharing responsibility for these outcomes. Students should not be designated "special education students" who fall only under the purview of special education teachers, with other students labeled "general education students" under the purview of general education teachers. Instead, educators must see the education of all students as their shared responsibility.

Two other dimensions of RTI are (a) using learning rates and levels of performance as the primary information regarding decision making about students with or at risk for disabilities, and (b) deciding intervention intensity and duration based on student responses to tiers of intervention (Dykeman, 2006; NASDSE, 2006). These dimensions align with the second recommendation of the Presidential Commission, which stresses preventing student failure. By assessing student outcomes early and often, and using these assessments to craft changes in instruction and delivery to accommodate for student differences, RTI seeks to avert the traditional "wait until the student fails" approach.

These two dimensions of RTI—using learning rates and levels of performance to guide decisions, and determining intervention intensity and duration based on student responses to tiered interventions—mean that special education service delivery does not begin when a student is formally assessed and found to have a disability. Rather, adjustments and accommodations are made early on when a student struggles. Teachers provide multiple interventions grounded in student-level data and tailored to meet individual students' needs. If lower tier interventions fail to work, a student moves to higher tiers. Dykeman (2006) explains that:

> RTI can be used as a pre-referral intervention strategy prior to any decision about special education eligibility. If successful, pre-referral interventions identify a suc-

cessful strategy that meets the child's academic needs and, therefore, absolves the need for eligibility determination. If unsuccessful, RTI provides documented data useful when deciding special education eligibility. (p. 268)

Thus, the emphasis in RTI on the delivery of tiered interventions and monitoring of student responses to these interventions represents a significant shift in focus of special education service delivery.

Service Delivery in Catholic Schools

Closing the gap between what is espoused (inclusive service delivery) and what is practiced (segregatory service delivery) is problematic in the Catholic schools as well as the public sector. Like their public counterparts, Catholic schools have historically struggled to serve all students. Yet Catholic schools have not always embraced a mission to meet all students' special needs. In a publication of the National Catholic Office for Persons with Disabilities, Bishop (1997) captures this:

> The development and education of children who are disabled has long been seen as the responsibility of the public school system and, more exclusively, the special education school programs of public schools. Catholic school inclusion calls educators back to their roots of caring for all children. (p. 4)

Shaughnessy (2005) cautions that Catholic schools hold neither a legal obligation nor the resource capacity to do so: "Catholic schools are not required to meet every need of every child. Most Catholic schools are not equipped to offer all educational services to everyone" (p. 139). Yet, as suggested in the earlier discussion of Catholic social teachings, the philosophy of Catholic schools compels them to strive to serve traditionally marginalized students. Shaughnessy puts this obligation in blunt terms regarding students with special needs:

> Special needs children and adolescents are certainly worthy of the Catholic Church's time and attention. It is a sad reality that only a few schools and parishes make adequate provisions for meeting the needs of such children. As persons striving to live in harmony with the Gospel, all involved in Catholic education are bound to do their utmost to assist students with special needs. (p. 142)

Recently Catholic schools have focused more intensively on this (Scanlan, in press-a; USCCB, 2002). Catholic schools serve students with special needs in all disability areas, and approximately 7% of students in Catholic schools have diagnosed special needs (Bimonte, 2006). Bimonte reports an increase in the number of Catholic schools that are explicitly developing service delivery mechanisms for students with diagnosed special needs. For instance, Bimonte states: "Almost 42% of the schools had a resource teacher paid by the school to assist children with special needs—up 8% from 2003. These resource teachers assisted an average of 23 students each week" (p. 33). Bimonte also notes a "significant increase in the percentage of students classified with physical disabilities, autism, and emotional/behavioral disabilities compared to 2000-2001" (p. 33).

Catholic Schools Pursuing Inclusive Service Delivery

Some evidence exists that Catholic schools are progressing toward service delivery that is inclusive. As Bishop (1997) asserts, inclusive service delivery is the appropriate model for Catholic schools: "Inclusion, defined as an approach to educating all individuals with and without disabilities in the regular classroom, is in sync with the concept of total Catholic education in its concern for the total development of all children" (p. 1). Select Catholic school systems are striving to more effectively serve students with disabilities by employing teacher assistants (Archdiocese of St. Louis Catholic Education Office, 2003a, 2003b; Long, Brown, & Nagy-Rado, 2007) and consultants (DeFiore, 2006).

Evidence suggests that while Catholic schools are paying more attention to serving students with special needs than they have previously, these services are expanding in an uneven fashion. Durow (2007) reports that the espoused missions of Catholic schools tend toward inclusion of students with disabilities, but that practices are inconsistent across schools. Gray and Gautier's (2006) research on trends in Catholic elementary and secondary schools suggests limitations in the attitudes of educational leaders in Catholic schools toward including students with disabilities. They note that 31% of school leaders say their school is very able to provide a welcoming environment to such students (another 40% say their school is somewhat able to do so). Complicating this, only 10% of these same leaders strongly agree that their school is able to accommodate students with special needs and/or disabilities, and nearly half (47%) disagree with this. At the district level, over half (51%) of the superintendents disagreed with the statement that schools are able to accommodate students with special needs and/or disabilities, and only 5% agree very much with this statement.

To be sure, the pursuit of inclusive service delivery in Catholic schools is fraught with barriers. According to Durow (2007), "the most significant barriers to improved service of students with special needs in Catholic schools were reported as inadequate funding, insufficient teacher preparation and confidence, inaccessible buildings, and inconsistent commitment from parishes and boards" (p. 487). Often families of students requiring extra services are required to pay supplemental fees (Powell, 2004). In other cases, the lack of ongoing professional development, resources, and support in curriculum and instruction hinders efforts toward inclusion (Bello, 2004; O'Shea & O'Shea, 1998).

Complicating the development of inclusive service delivery models for students with special needs in Catholic schools are the inconsistent effects of Section 504 and IDEA. While these encourage inclusive service delivery in public settings, Catholic schools, as private institutions, experience these laws somewhat differently. If a Catholic school receives any direct federal funds, they are subject to Section 504.

Frequently Catholic schools receive indirect resources from the federal government, such as Title Services. As McDonald (2005) states, "under NCLB and IDEA, services are provided to students and teachers; no money is channeled to schools" (p. 102). Whether or not the participation of students in federally funded programs subjects a school to Section 504 is a disputed issue (Mawdsley, 2000).

Under Section 504, Catholic schools are required to make reasonable accommodations if a student has made a demand for this (Russo et al., 2002). They can be excused from making accommodations on one of three grounds: (a) the change would fundamentally alter the nature of a program, (b) the change would be unduly burdensome financially, or (c) the accommodation would result in substantial risk of injury to somebody, either the individual and/or others (Mawdsley, 2000). Schools may operate separate, comparable classes for students with disabilities if "education in a traditional setting cannot be accomplished satisfactorily" (p. 202). Additionally, the schools may charge additional fees for services that are substantially more costly than "supplementary aids and services provided in the regular school environment" (p. 202).

Essentially, Section 504 could be read to create a number of barriers for students with disabilities in Catholic schools. First, the schools have a disincentive to identify students with disabilities, because they are only required to make accommodations for students who request this. Second, these are excused from accommodating such students if this would be too "burdensome." Accordingly, schools are dissuaded from developing service delivery systems to meet the needs of students with disabilities, since so long as these systems are undeveloped, the schools can claim that their development would be burdensome. Finally, if Catholic schools do accept and accommodate students with disabilities, the schools can charge the students extra fees for doing so. Thus, while Section 504 does directly apply to Catholic schools, it does not encourage them to proactively develop inclusive service delivery.

The impact of IDEA on Catholic schools is starkly different than Section 504. IDEA encourages Catholic schools to identify students with disabilities in order to secure their proportionate share of the federal dollars (McDonald, 2007b). While an individual student with a diagnosed disability who is parentally placed in a private school does not have an entitlement to special services, the private school does have a right to a proportional amount of federal funding for special education funding (McDonald, 2005). The more parentally-placed private school children with disabilities identified by Catholic schools, the greater the proportion of funds the school district must expend on services for them. McDonald (2005) explains this process:

> Private school officials consult with the local school district (LEA) about the types of services, programs and materials that would help to meet the unique needs of their students and teachers. The LEA provides and pays for special teachers, non-ideological materials or professional development programs agreed upon in the consultation process. (p. 102)

However, while Catholic school students with individualized education programs (IEP) are afforded the same federal protections, they may not insist that services be provided within the Catholic school setting. As Doyle (2004) states, while IDEA is both an education law and a civil rights guarantee, "children attending private schools who are suspected of having a disability have fewer rights and protections under IDEA" (p. 70). Mawdsley (2000) points out that while an IEP may be implemented in whole or in part in a Catholic school setting, the "responsibility for appropriate implementation of the IEP always remains with the public school district" (p. 244). In a consultation process, public and private school officials negotiate to determine which children are served with IDEA funds. Doyle explains that "to receive a free, appropriate public education the parents of a private school child usually must transfer the child with a disability into the public school system" (p. 70). Thus, while Catholic school students do have a right to a proportionate share of federal funds provided through IDEA, they do not have a right to FAPE (Mawdsley, 2000; Russo, Massucci, & Osborne, 2000). Public school personnel are permitted, but not required, to provide service delivery to students with disabilities at Catholic schools. Russo et al. (2000) clarify that IDEA regulations "make it clear that children in religious schools are entitled to receive some special education services, [but] on the other hand, they contain funding restrictions that may actually mean that these children will receive fewer services" (p. 376). Mawdsley (2000) describes the dilemma this leaves to families of students with disabilities:

> As long as the districts provide FAPE they have control over special education resources and can determine where they will be invested. For parents who want their children with disabilities in a nonpublic, especially religious, school, the choice is a hard one. Unless the public school services under the IEP are inappropriate to provide FAPE, parents will either have to fund the nonpublic cost on their own or leave the child in the public school. (p. 249)

IDEA can therefore be read to create quite different barriers to Catholic school students with disabilities than Section 504. On one hand, IDEA encourages Catholic schools to identify students with disabilities in order that they can receive some funded services from the local public school district. On the other hand, the way these services will be delivered is typically in a segregated manner by removing the children from their classrooms to attend pull-out programming by public school personnel. Whether this programming is on-site in another room, in a van parked outside the school, or at the local public school, the effect is the same: students with disabilities will likely receive service delivery in the least integrative setting.

To recap, legal and educational scholarship on service delivery suggests a strong rationale for inclusive service delivery models. Inclusive service delivery is consistent with the Catholic social teachings emphasizing human dignity, the common good, and a preferential option for the marginalized. Yet educational practices in general, and in Catholic schools in particular, are not consistently oriented toward inclusive service delivery.

Integrated Comprehensive Services

In the previous two chapters we have established the foundation for critically reviewing service delivery models for students with special needs in light of Catholic social teaching (CST). This chapter describes a service delivery model that is aligned with CST: Integrated Comprehensive Services, or ICS (Frattura & Capper, 2007a). After providing an overview of ICS, the chapter concludes with a discussion of legal, policy, and resource implications of ICS in Catholic school settings.

Overview of ICS

Frattura and Capper (Capper et al., 2000; Frattura & Capper, 2007a, 2007b) have articulated the most thorough and comprehensive model for inclusive service delivery in what they call Integrated Comprehensive Services, or ICS. While other models of inclusive service delivery exist (e.g., Ferguson, Kozleski, Fulton, & Smith, 2005), I argue that ICS provides an approach that comports well with CST, and thus lends itself well to Catholic school contexts. Building on earlier work (Prater, 2003), Frattura and Capper argue that educational leaders who are oriented toward social justice must approach service delivery to students across all dimensions of diversity in an inclusive manner. At the heart of ICS is the notion that inclusive service delivery is the most effective and socially just approach to educating all students. Frattura and Capper demonstrate that segregated programs deliver support in a selective manner that divides students and limits schools from enhancing the capacity of all educators to serve diverse learners. Inclusive service delivery depends on general education teachers developing skills and strategies to serve all students (Villa, Thousand, Meyers, & Nevin, 1996). This involves general educators recognizing that they are responsible for all students, including those who are struggling in certain manners. Key factors impacting educators' attitudes toward inclusion and heterogeneous classrooms include administrative support, time to collaborate, and experience with students with severe and profound disabilities (Harris, Kaff, Anderson, & Knackendoffel, 2007; Rose & Meyer, 2002).

As discussed in chapter 3, programmatic approaches to service delivery separate students into discrete groups. Students in poverty receive Title I services, students with diagnosed disabilities receive special education services, and students who are English language learners receive bilingual education services. By contrast, ICS explicitly rejects this programmatic approach and instead incorporates the principles of universal design for learning for all students (Frattura & Capper, 2007a). These principles promote conceptualizing teaching and learning environments in manners that they are made accessible to a wide array of learners, with multiple modes of presenting information, engaging learners, and allowing for the demonstration of knowledge. The ICS approach to service delivery emphasizes the prevention of student failure by building the capacity of all educators to teach to a range of diverse student strengths and needs. Thus, instead of creating an array of programs to intervene in response to student failure, this model focuses on how to proactively shape the curriculum and the teaching and learning environment of the school so that the needs of all students can be met in heterogeneous settings. Instead of grouping select students into specific programs (i.e., students with disabilities into certain rooms, students who are English language learners into other rooms), students are placed in their natural proportions within classrooms throughout the school. This creates the structural expectation that all educators are responsible for serving all students. Frattura and Capper (2007a) explain how the role of support staff shifts in this ICS context:

> The goal of support staff becomes to initially support students in these settings, but ultimately to build the general educator capacity to teach to a range of students. In ICS, over time, one goal of support staff is to fade their involvement in the classroom because the general classroom teacher has strengthened her teaching and learning strategies to meet a range of student needs. (p. 17)

In this manner, ICS seeks to break the cycle where the limited expertise of educators effectively confines student placement options to select individuals, further limiting the development of expertise in other educators to serve these students.

Cornerstones of ICS

The four "cornerstones" of ICS, Frattura and Capper (2007a) explain, are (a) establishing core principles that focus on equity, (b) locating and arranging educational services equitably, (c) building teacher capacity and curriculum and instruction to provide all students access to high-quality teaching and learning, and (d) establishing the resources and policies that will sustain these changes. These cornerstones have considerable overlap with the values of CST, particularly as discussed in chapter 2, emphasizing human dignity, the common good, and a preferential option for the marginalized. These four cornerstones are illustrated in Figure 1.

The first cornerstone of ICS is a focus on equity. A core component of Frattura and Capper's (2007a) presentation of ICS is the principle of equity. In Catholic school communities this is broadened somewhat by placing as foundational the core values of CST: human dignity, the common good, and a preferential option for the marginalized. Ensuring that all students are welcomed into the heart of the school

1: Core Principles
- Human dignity
- Common good
- Preferential option for the marginalized

2: Equitable Structures
- Team supports
- Family engagement
- Practices of recruitment and retention

3: Access to High-Quality Teaching and Learning
- Building capacity of each teacher to serve a range of students
- Crafting the teaching and learning environment to support students with special needs
- Horizontal, vertical, & diagonal supports

4: Policy and Resource Mechanisms
- Policies and resources aligned with CST
- Policies and resources coordinated in support of ICS

Figure 1. Four cornerstones of Integrated Comprehensive Services (ICS) infused with Catholic social teaching (CST). Adapted from Frattura and Capper (2007a).

community, not pushed to the periphery, operationalizes the value of the human dignity of all. The value of the common good is manifest when educators recognize and treat as valuable the multiple dimensions of diversity in the school community.

As educators ally themselves with students who are struggling they are making a preferential option for the marginalized. Frattura and Capper (2007a) emphasize that school leaders need to not only cultivate these beliefs, but have both the knowledge and the skills to act upon these beliefs. Additionally, these leaders should be candid about their own limitations and push themselves to deepen their practices. Frattura and Capper (2007a) identify as a final characteristic of these leaders the commitment to continually develop and sustain an ethical core. This is essential to empower these leaders to withstand countervailing pressures. This emphasis aligns well with the importance of contemplative practice in transformational leadership in Catholic schools (Schuttloffel, 2008).

The second cornerstone to ICS is establishing structures that are equitable. Frattura and Capper (2007a) suggest that developing and implementing ICS depends upon shared decision making, strategically assigning staff to maximize student learning, and strategically assigning students into classes that "maximize student opportunities to learn in heterogeneous groups, and that thus create the conditions for optimal student learning" (p. 61). They detail processes for cultivating building-level and district-level teams comprised of administrators, teachers, staff, parents, and students to support these structures (Frattura & Capper, 2007b). Essentially, this operationalizes the distribution of leadership and decision making around service delivery broadly throughout the school community across multiple constituents, practices supported by other literature in the field, including Catholic school communities (e.g., Drago-Severson, 2007; Fitzgibbons, Mahon, & Maus, 2008; McCullough, Graf, Leung, Stroud, & Orlando, 2008). In particular, Catholic schools have a strong tradition of recognizing parents and families as core partners in the education of each child.

A key concept that Frattura and Capper (2007a) emphasize here is placing students in natural proportions. This means that the general demographics of the school community are reflected throughout subsets within the school community. As applied to students with special needs, school leaders must ensure that these students are not disproportionately over represented or underrepresented in certain classrooms, extracurricular activities, or other areas. In the Catholic school context, structures to support natural proportions must start with recruitment practices and retention practices oriented toward welcoming students with special needs. While public schools operate within districts that provide external supports for schools to accept these students, Catholic schools are much more independent. Accordingly, without deliberate effort, Catholic schools typically lack structures that support the recruitment and retention of students with special needs. Examples of such supports are increasingly apparent in Catholic school communities.

The third cornerstone of ICS focuses on building the capacity of all educators in the school to create teaching and learning for all students. Frattura and Capper (2007a) argue that building the expertise of one another compels teachers to "no longer concede or defer their power or expertise to so-called 'experts' down the hall, at another school, or in another district" (p. 117). Instead, they explain, "Educators must view their primary roles as developing the capacity of each other to teach to a range of students in the classroom" (p. 117). Concomitant to building the capacity of teachers, ICS emphasizes constructing schedules, teacher placement, student movement, and curriculum with a constant focus on raising all student achievement to grade level standards and beyond. As mentioned above, in ICS the principle of universal design guides the development of curriculum and instruction that will serve the diversity of learning needs in heterogeneous classrooms, and the scheduling of teacher placement and student movement emphasizes student needs over the convenience of adults.

In the Catholic school context, an additional component to this cornerstone of building the capacity of educators in the school involves cultivating horizontal, vertical, and diagonal relationships of support. Fullan (2004, 2006) describes systemic improvement as scaffolded through horizontal (teacher to teacher, principal to principal) and vertical (between teacher and principal, or principal and superintendent) connections within and among schools. Fullan argues that educators benefit from building connections between their work within their own schools and similar work at other schools and at the systems level. To effectively pursue systemic change, school leaders must develop experience and expertise linking to multiple levels of the system by fostering these connections. To support the capacity in Catholic schools, which are more independent and autonomous than public sector schools, these horizontal and vertical connections are particularly important. A third dimension that is key for Catholic schools can be termed "diagonal" connections. These are connections across sectors, such as to public school districts and to private service providers. In short, this cornerstone must be expanded in the Catholic school context to emphasize these horizontal, vertical, and diagonal relationships.

Finally, the fourth cornerstone of ICS is coordinating resources and policies to implement and sustain the changes. Frattura and Capper (2007a) go to lengths to demonstrate that the reallocation of funding and resources allows schools to move from program-based, segregatory service delivery to ICS. They emphasize that ICS reduces "the duplication of staff and materials between schools and programs and across programs" (p. 195) through specific strategies, such as pursuing dual certification for faculty (e.g., special education or bilingual certification alongside grade level or subject area certification), or streamlining referral-to-service forms and processes. In the Catholic school context, these policies and resource mechanisms must be aligned with the core values of Catholic social teaching.

Beyond Pre-Referral Strategies
As this brief overview of the four cornerstones suggest, ICS differs in substantive ways from pre-referral strategies to reforming special education service delivery. Pre-referral interventions, increasingly mandated (43%) or recommended (29%) by states, (Kovaleski, Tucker, & Stevens, 1996; Whitfield, 1996), are team-based strategies to intervene to meet student needs prior to a formal special education evaluation. Such interventions emphasize building the capacity of classroom teachers to meet these needs within the general education setting. One prominent pre-referral model is the Instructional Support Team, which gained popularity in Pennsylvania in the 1990s (Fleming, Doerries, Stickney, & Spital, 2002) and has subsequently been adopted by other states, such as Virginia (Hartman & Fay, 1996; Kovaleski, Gickling, Morrow, & Swank, 1999). When implemented with strong leadership, extensive data-driven decision making, and ongoing strategic adaptation driven by a key teacher, the Instructional Support Team model is an effective remedial intervention for raising student performance and reducing referrals to special education (Rosenfield, 1987). A related pre-referral model is called Instrucational Consultation (Chalfant, Pysh, & Moultrie, 1979). These models build from earlier scholarship promoting collaborative work between general and special educators to address the needs of students who are struggling (Gravois & Rosenfield, 2006). These approaches are also shown to reduce the disproportionate placement of students of color in special education (Hale et al., 2006; Martinez et al., 2006; NASDSE, 2006).

ICS is both congruent with and distinct from the Response to Intervention (RTI) approach described in chapter 3. As Martinez and colleagues (2006) explain, "RTI is a methodology that promotes successful school outcomes for all students through the systematic integration of services in general and special education" (p. 5). The emphasis on differentiating instruction and assessment and early interventions to provide remediation align with the cornerstones of ICS, especially the third cornerstone, which focuses on building teacher capacity and curriculum and instruction to provide all students access to high-quality teaching and learning. Both RTI and ICS prioritize identifying students who are not mastering basic skills and immediately responding with more intensive learning supports. Targeted supports complement the core curriculum and require teachers to monitor student progress.

RTI, however, does not necessarily transform the fundamental service delivery structure as much as ICS. As some have noted, RTI implies structural changes. The National Association of State Directors of Special Education (Guerra, 2000) describes RTI as "more than prereferral services; it is a comprehensive service delivery system that requires significant changes in how a school serves all students" (p. 2). Yet RTI does not require structural change beyond introducing tiers of interventions for students at risk for special education referral. Thus, schools can adopt reforms of RTI while leaving the programmatic approach of service delivery in place, albeit buffered. By contrast, the core principles of ICS challenge the inherent structuring of service delivery in a manner where students who are struggling are divided into separate programs. Instead of focusing on discrete groups of students in isolation, ICS directs school leaders to approach service delivery across the multiple dimensions of diversity in the student body. Further, instead of focusing primarily on intervening in response to student failure (the approach of RTI), ICS emphasizes designing this service delivery with the primary aim of preventing student failure. In short, by addressing the school as a system, ICS is a holistic approach to reform that is congruent with, but extending beyond, RTI.

Policy Implications of ICS

Integrated Comprehensive Services is a model that provides Catholic schools with a principled approach to service delivery to students with special needs in a manner consistent with Catholic social teaching. As discussed in chapter 2, the Catholic identity of Catholic schools is nonnegotiable. The authenticity of Catholic schools in understanding, explaining, and supporting their unique religious and educational mission is central to their future. Catholic schools defy CST when they fail to strive diligently to affirm the human dignity of all, promote the common good, and make a preferential option for the marginalized. Barton (2000) captures this in lucid language: "The question is not simple 'to include or not to include,' but rather, 'Can Catholic schools not be inclusive and still be truly Catholic?' In other words, does the idea of Catholic identity necessarily embody inclusion?" (p. 329). Fundamentally, ICS provides Catholic schools with clear direction in developing policies that maintain this identity by aligning service delivery practices with CST.

As illustrated in Figure 1, ICS and CST overlap in many ways. First, CST's emphasis on the dignity of each individual is directly reflected in Frattura and Capper's (2007a) consistent emphasis that all students are learners who belong in the school community. The positive anthropology of the human person recognizes that all members of the human family are made in the image and likeness of God. School policies reflect this to the degree to which they structure the teaching and learning environment of the school to welcome the multiple dimensions of diversity manifest in this human family. Second, CST's emphasis on the common good parallels the emphasis in ICS that programmatic approaches to service delivery isolate and segregate students who struggle. Third, CST's emphasis on a preferential option for the marginalized echoes Frattura and Capper's discussion of leaders in ICS as "advocates for students who struggle in their school" (p. 30). This preferential option for the marginalized is a profoundly countercultural message that Catholic schools struggle to operationalize. ICS can help school leaders move in practical manners toward fostering schools that effectively place the needs of the most disadvantaged at the forefront.

In addition, ICS aligns well with the emphasis in CST on subsidiarity. As described earlier (see Table 1, p. 12), subsidiarity emphasizes that decisions should be made by those closest to the consequences. ICS emphasizes that those closest to the child need to be invested and involved in strategizing about the education of the child. The classroom teacher cannot simply rely on the special educator to accommodate the special needs. Rather, the classroom teacher needs to be empowered to play an active role. The specific delivery of educational services cannot be divorced from the basic community of the classroom, but must be conceptualized and carried out as an integral component to this classroom.

Despite its secular formulation, the ICS approach integrates the values of CST and applies them to the educational context of Catholic schools. Specifically, ICS provides Catholic school principals, teachers, and board members a lens through which to critically analyze how they approach student recruitment, retention, scheduling, and service delivery, as well as practices of hiring, staffing, and professional development. In this manner, ICS builds on Long and Shuttloffel's (2006) rationale for including students with special needs by articulating a service delivery system. The lack of relevant policies in these areas around service delivery to students with special needs is a significant barrier preventing Catholic schools from better serving such students. While Frattura and Capper's (2007a) approach is crafted to directly apply to public school contexts, the ICS approach applies directly to Catholic schooling as well. In many ways ICS provides Catholic schools with a yardstick by which to measure the congruence of their practices with CST.

Legal Implications of ICS

The model of ICS provides Catholic schools with a way to navigate the contradictory pressures of federal laws and regulations on developing service delivery models to serve students with special needs. As discussed in chapter 3, Section 504 gives incentives to Catholic schools to not develop comprehensive service delivery plans to address a diversity of learners, and IDEA encourages Catholic schools to label students with disabilities and then deliver services to them in a segregatory manner. ICS serves as a compass to wade through these incongruous pressures in a manner consistent with CST.

In response to Section 504, ICS directs Catholic schools to develop inclusive service delivery systems for students with special needs, proactively working to build the capacity to make accommodations for diverse learners within heterogeneous settings. To the degree that Catholic schools take to heart their commitments to recognizing the dignity of all, promoting the common good, and giving preference to the marginalized, they will design programming to provide accommodations for students with disabilities and undiagnosed special needs. Thus, what could be taken as a disincentive to identify students with disabilities is replaced by the acknowl-edgement of the value of embracing in the school community individuals reflecting multiple dimensions of diversity (Long & Schuttloffel, 2006). The development of effective and inclusive service delivery, as outlined in ICS, reduces the likelihood that such accommodations will be burdensome or be only available to families able to pay additional fees. In other words, ICS guides Catholic schools to embrace both the spirit and letter of Section 504.

In response to IDEA, ICS implies Catholic schools should be diligent in iden-tifying students with disabilities in order to access all available resources to allow them to serve these students. This compels administrators at both the school and diocesan levels to foster strong working relationships with public school personnel in the Child Find process in order to effectively and cooperatively craft systems of allocating appropriate funds for students with disabilities in Catholic schools. In addition to maximizing resources, ICS guides these administrators to ensure that services are delivered, as IDEA directs, in the least restrictive environment. This means delivering these services within the Catholic school and in integrated, het-erogeneous settings.

As noted in the earlier discussion of IDEA, control for deciding how services are delivered rests in the hands of the public school district personnel. Thus, prudent Catholic school leaders, both at the school or diocesan levels, must cultivate strong working relationships with their colleagues in the local public school system so that they are able to secure these federal funds in a manner that allows for the most flex-ible service delivery possible. Public school personnel are more apt to collaborate with Catholic school leaders in this manner as they see behavior that belies the myth of Catholic schools simply creaming off the top performing students and relegating all students who struggle academically, behaviorally, or emotionally to the public school system (Baker, 1999; Baker & Riordan, 1998, 1999; Lawrence, 2000; O'Keefe & Murphy, 2000; Riordan, 2000).

Resource Implications of ICS

Finally, and perhaps most importantly, the resource implications of ICS ensure that Catholic schools build their capacity to allow them to strengthen their Catholic identity by effectively serving students with special needs. As discussed in chapter 3, federal resources are garnered through diligently engaging with public schools in the Child Find process and guiding the proportionate share of these dollars to service delivery that integrates students with disabilities into the school community. Moreover, embracing ICS allows Catholic schools and dioceses to coordinate their efforts in efficiently guiding extant resources and in attracting additional community resources to better meet the needs of all students.

Catholic schools with well-articulated systems of service delivery are positioned to strategically employ current resources to meet the needs of all students. As Frattura and Capper (2007a) demonstrate, the ICS model builds the internal capacity of schools to serve students with special needs by increasing the skills of all educators to differentiate instruction as well as by replacing disparate programming with flexible, heterogeneous student grouping. The services that students need, such as remediation in reading, are not delivered in the resource room down the hall, or the van parked outside, but instead in the classroom. Support personnel, such as the special education teacher or the reading resource teacher, work both directly with students in the classroom as well as with the classroom teachers to help them better meet the needs of students who are struggling.

The literature shows that Catholic schools that are crafting inclusive service delivery models for students with special needs already demonstrate some of these practices in resource allocation (Long et al., 2007). For instance, the Archdiocese of Washington, DC, is collaborating to educate consultative special education teachers with dual certifications (Crowley & Wall, 2007) as well as teacher assistants (Lawrence-Brown & Muschaweck, 2004). Other Catholic schools have benefited from professional development aimed at collaborative teaming. In another example, for over a decade the Archdiocese of St. Louis has used school-based learning consultants to help teachers and administrators meet the needs of students with special needs (Archdiocese of St. Louis Catholic Education Office, 2003a). O'Shea and O'Shea (1998) found in their study of an inclusive Catholic high school that consistent and persistent professional development, teacher ownership of accommodations, and collaboration with families promote the success of inclusive service delivery.

ICS also positions Catholic schools to attract new resources to build their capacity to deliver services to students with special needs. This is not a new phenomenon, as Catholic schools seeking to effectively serve traditionally marginalized students consistently take innovative approaches to fundraising and resource attainment (O'Keefe et al., 2004; O'Keefe & Murphy, 2000). The literature shows that Catholic schools working to serve students with special needs frequently attract external funding to support their service delivery systems (Lefevere, 2005; Powell, 2004). Parents and principals are often the strongest champions for inclusive service delivery, effectively leveraging community and diocesan resources toward this end (Scanlan, in press-a). ICS provides schools and dioceses with clear language with which to approach private funding agencies and donors to allow them to bring into the school new resources for student services and professional development.

Finally, Catholic schools with underdeveloped service delivery systems are uniquely positioned to move toward ICS. Unlike their public school counterparts, most Catholic schools do not need to radically transform existing programmatic approaches to service delivery for students with special needs. Lacking any can actually serve as an advantage to these schools. Due to their private nature and their dependence on attracting students and families over other private as well as public schools, Catholic schools generally have been forced to pursue educational innovations and reform strategies that use resources efficiently. Building inclusive service delivery allows Catholic schools to attract and serve students that they currently leave out. ICS provides a strategy for schools to build such service delivery in a manner that uses resources efficiently, expanding the capacity of the entire school community to welcome and educate such students, and aligning the service delivery with the basic values of CST (Weaver & Landers, 2000).

Inclusive Service Delivery Across Other Dimensions of Diversity

In this fifth chapter, I extend the examination of inclusive service delivery across other dimensions of diversity. In the previous two chapters I have focused on how one particular model of inclusive service delivery, Integrated Comprehensive Services (ICS) can help Catholic schools more effectively welcome students with special needs. The phrase "students with special needs" is an umbrella term. It includes students with diagnosed disabilities as well as those facing other barriers to success but lacking a formal disability label. Now, we turn to apply this model to other traditionally marginalized students. In this chapter I examine ways that ICS provides Catholic school leaders a comprehensive model for operationalizing Catholic social teachings across other dimensions of diversity, including poverty, race, religion, and home language.

The model of ICS pioneered by Frattura and Capper (2007a) is explicitly expansive. It is not limited to students with special needs, but instead provides school leaders a framework for approaching the multiple dimensions of diversity that are manifest in our increasingly pluralistic student bodies. The basic premise is that services should be delivered to all students in a manner that integrates them into the community, builds on their strengths, and promotes their growth. Ameliorating barriers to inclusion should not be an afterthought, but a design feature. This is analogous to how the principles of universal design are transforming curriculum development and delivery (Pisha & Coyne, 2001; Rose & Meyer, 2002). Instead of creating lessons for some "typical learner" and then seeking to modify these lessons to accommodate the diversity of learners that are present, educators are striving to articulate both specific teaching targets and flexible ways to reach them (Tomlinson & McTighe, 2006). This principle of universal design directs the school community to continually seek to improve how learning goals are accessible by individuals with wide differences in their abilities to see, hear, speak, move, read, write, understand English, attend, organize, engage, and remember (Rose & Meyer, 2002). As argued in chapter 4, the creation of separate programs to provide specific services to address these differences within specific students is inefficient and ineffective. By contrast, an integrated approach considers how multifarious factors (e.g., classroom design, teacher placement, professional development, scheduling, and student groupings) can work in concert to create a school community where all members are integral and integrated.

While Frattura and Capper (2007a) emphasize this expansive approach, my focus thus far has been to specifically develop ICS as a means for approaching inclusive service delivery for students with special needs in Catholic schools. I now move to examine a more expansive approach to inclusive service delivery to guide Catholic school leaders in integrating the values of Catholic social teaching, especially human dignity, the common good, and a preferential option for the marginalized, into the policies and practices across multiple dimensions of diversity.

As presented at the outset of this book, Catholic, which signifies "universal," impels Catholic schools to open their doors to welcome all who seek to enter. Making Catholic schools accessible is both a core challenge and a fundamental obligation (USCCB, 2005a). Although Catholic social teaching directs adherents to look across multiple dimensions of diversity, educators in all sectors, public as well as private, often emphasize select dimensions while ignoring others. For instance, school leaders might focus efforts at improving service to students with special needs while neglecting service delivery to students who are English language learners. An expansive approach to service delivery protects against this tendency.

In this chapter I will briefly describe two ways to operationalize an expansive approach to service delivery in Catholic schools. First, I describe how Care Teams, which are gaining popularity in Catholic schools, provide an example of a structure to build inclusive service delivery. Second, I discuss how to approach service delivery for students who are English language learners in a manner congruent with inclusive service delivery.

Care Teams in Catholic Schools

A core design feature of ICS in particular, and school improvement strategies in general, is the use of teams within schools. Teams are present in many school communities and vary tremendously (D. W. Johnson & Johnson, 2009). Their focus can range from discrete tasks (e.g., reviewing and improving the math curriculum across an elementary school) to general duties (e.g., a broader curriculum development team). Educational literature supports the use of teaming in schools for a variety of aims, such as improving teaching and learning (Thousand, Villa, & Nevin, 2006), guiding special education decision making (Bahr & Kovaleski, 2006), or reforming bilingual service delivery (Bahamonde & Friend, 1999). Literature suggests that Catholic school communities effectively use a variety of teaming approaches (Drago-Severson, 2007; Durow, 2007; Fitzgibbons et al., 2008; McCullough et al., 2008). Teams can be ongoing or ad hoc, and membership often includes combinations of administrators, teachers, staff, parents and caregivers, students, and community members.

Frattura and Capper (2007a) describe a range of teams that comprise an integrated, comprehensive approach to service delivery, including a School Planning Team, School Service Delivery Team, Grade Level Design Teams, and District Level Service Delivery Team. Yet in the Catholic school context, with smaller schools and site-based management, this range of teams is typically not feasible or necessary. However, one type of team that is emerging as a popular model in the Catholic school context is a Care Team (Fitzgibbons et al., 2008). While an extensive description of the Care Team process is beyond the scope of this text and is provided elsewhere (e.g., Fitzgibbons et al.), I will briefly describe how Care Teams are one component of operationalizing inclusive service delivery.

Care Teams are emerging as a specific way that Catholic school communities organize themselves to better serve students who are struggling (Fitzgibbons et al., 2008). Care Teams are groups of key educators in the school community who regularly meet to address situations in which students are facing difficulties. These difficulties are typically multifaceted, involving academic, social, behavioral, and emotional components, and they frequently traverse home-school boundaries. Fitzgibbons and colleagues explain the basic process:

> Care Teams operate with a simple, case-management process. Any school professional may refer any…student to the Care Team. The staff person making the referral does not have to be a Care Team member. Referrals can be made for any serious concerns that impact the school environment, whether academic, behavioral, emotional, familial, or substance-related. (p. 21)

Membership varies from school to school. Typically, the school administrator is always a member of the Care Team. Select school personnel, including teachers and support staff, form the core membership of the Care Teams, but their selection varies based on the particular needs of the school. In addition, successful Care Teams frequently contract with an external consultant to both provide this training and to serve as a member of the team. Such a consultant can bring specific expertise (such as mental health training) and objectivity to the process (Fitzgibbons et al., 2008). In the best cases, these Care Team members are specifically trained to perform their duties. This training addresses a number of topics, ranging from a systems approach to understanding family functioning, the continuum of childhood mental health disorders, disciplinary and classroom management tactics, and ethical issues related to Care Team work (Fitzgibbons et al.).

As a group dedicated to responding in a timely manner to student struggles across a range of areas, Care Teams create a practical way for Catholic school communities to take an expansive approach to inclusive service delivery. Care Teams serve as an organizational conduit toward systematically addressing students' struggles in a timely, balanced manner. In contrast to the narrower discussion of inclusive service delivery and Integrated Comprehensive Services (Frattura & Capper, 2007a) in the previous chapter, which focused specifically on students with special needs, Care Teams consider students' struggles in multiple areas, including academic, social, behavioral, and emotional. As such, Care Teams illustrate an expansive and holistic approach for Catholic schools to increase access and reduce barriers to traditionally marginalized students.

Service Delivery for Students Who Are English Language Learners

In addition to implementing Care Teams, a second way to operationalize inclusive service delivery across multiple dimensions of diversity is in service delivery for students who are English language learners (ELL). Catholic school leaders need practical strategies to welcome students who are English language learners. Frequently our schools have not articulated our approaches to these students, or have done so in a piecemeal fashion. In this section we will examine how Integrated Comprehensive Services (ICS; Frattura & Capper, 2007a), implemented in Catholic school communities and grounded in Catholic social teaching, provides direction for developing coherent strategies to serve students who are ELL.

Responding to linguistic diversity is not new for many schools in the United States. Olneck (2004) reminds us that historically "American schools have, however reluctantly, always had to revise their practices and policies to accommodate immigrant languages, cultures, and identities, but their success in educating immigrant children has been uneven" (p. 399). Currently the linguistic diversity in our country is increasing at a remarkable rate. According to the National Center for Education Statistics (2004), among youth ages 5-24 "the percentage who were language minorities increased from 9 percent in 1979 to 17 percent in 1999" (p. iii). Over the last 2 decades of the 20th century the number of U.S. residents speaking a language other than English at home more than doubled (Crawford, 2002).

Catholic schools, many of which were founded to serve discrete communities of immigrant Catholics, are increasingly integrating students who are ELL into existing schools (Lawrence, 2000). While many of these families are of low socioeconomic status, making tuition a significant barrier to traditionally-financed Catholic schools, Lawrence emphasizes that in Catholic school communities, "obstacles or opportunities afforded by local school and parish environments seem just as important [as family income] in shaping their school-choice preferences and decisions" (p. 197). Foremost among these obstacles is the presence or absence of a well-formulated service delivery plan to meet these students' linguistic needs.

The inclusive approach to service delivery presented in this book, reflecting the values of Catholic social teaching (CST), provides direction to policies and practices to effectively serve students who are English language learners. CST directs schools to affirm the inherent dignity of each individual, including the linguistic and cultural heritage that they bring. The CST emphasis on the common good directs Catholic schools to see students who are ELL and their families as integral, valuable members of the broader school community. Additionally, the preferential option for the marginalized translates into proactively welcoming linguistically diverse students into Catholic school communities.

Generally speaking, these values have been consistently and clearly manifest in the Catholic Church's approach to immigrant communities (Lummert, 2000; Pontifical Council for Justice and Peace, 2004). Specifically looking at Catholic schools, however, these values are less readily apparent. Information on the numbers of students who are ELL in Catholic schools and the service delivery systems used with them is not typically gathered (Bimonte, 2006; Gray & Gautier, 2006; McDonald & Schultz, 2008).

The four cornerstones of Integrated Comprehensive Services (Frattura & Capper, 2007a), as described in chapter 4, provide guidance for school leaders striving to effectively serve students who are English language learners. I will apply each of these four cornerstones—(a) focusing on equity, (b) establishing equitable structures in educational services, (c) providing access to high-quality teaching and learning, and (d) implementing funding and policy mechanisms to support change—to service delivery for students who are ELL in Catholic school communities.

Cornerstone 1: Focusing on Equity

As emphasized earlier, the focus on equity in the cornerstone of ICS (Frattura & Capper, 2007a) can be broadened in the Catholic school context to three core values of Catholic social teaching: human dignity, the common good, and a preferential option for the marginalized. The mission and vision statements and philosophies of Catholic school communities frequently extol the value of each individual member of the school community, and emphasize partnering with families as the primary educators of the child. With regard to students who are ELL, these values need to be manifest by approaching linguistic diversity as an asset.

An asset-based approach to linguistic diversity treats the home language of the student as valuable. To contextualize this approach, consider the spectrum of options schools have for providing educational services to students who are ELL. Two broad categories to distinguish these options are English immersion and bilingual education. As Slavin and Cheung (2005) distinguish, "bilingual education differs fundamentally from English immersion in that it gives English language learners significant amounts of instruction in reading and/or other subjects in their native language" (p. 250). These two broad categories often frame the range of choices school leaders consider for how to respond to students who are ELL.

Ovando (2003) places these two categories—English immersion and bilingual education—on a continuum, identifying five types of programs running between the two, as illustrated in Table 2. While all categories share the goal of English proficiency, the maintenance of the home language (in this example, Spanish) is present in only two.

Ovando (2003) describes those that approach the development of this second language at the expense of the first language as "subtractive," and those that foster developing both the second and the native language as "additive" (p. 24). Subtractive approaches contribute to a loss of native-language literacy skills and limited bilingualism, while additive ones contribute to bilingualism and biliteracy. In other words, the three approaches on the left-hand side of Ovando's spectrum are subtractive, while the two on the right-hand side are additive. The goal of the first three approaches is solely English language development, while the goal of the final two approaches is bilingualism. These could be considered on a continuum from deficit-based to asset-based, as Table 3 illustrates.

Additive approaches to students who are ELL emphasize equity by treating the home language of the student as an asset, not a deficit. While school-specific factors shape the degree to which the school can functionally support the acquisition and development of the home language, the emphasis here is that the school affirms this language as valuable. Students who are ELL are much more apt to succeed when their language and culture are incorporated into the school and their parents and community are viewed as integral components of their education (Cummins, 1986).

Table 2				
Continuum of Approaches to Students Who Are ELL				
English immersion --Bilingual education				
English only	Transitional bilingual education "early-exit"	Transitional bilingual education "late-exit"	Maintenance/ developmental bilingual education	Two-way bilingual education
Instruction in English with English-as-a-Second-Language (ESL) support	Instruction in English and Spanish	Instruction in English and Spanish	Instruction in English and Spanish	Instruction in English and Spanish
Students who are ELL not segregated	Students who are ELL initially segregated, then mainstreamed in monolingual classes within 2 years	Students who are ELL initially segregated, then mainstreamed in monolingual classes significantly later	Students who are ELL initially segregated, then mainstreamed in monolingual classes significantly later	Students who are ELL not segregated

Table 3				
Distinctions Among Approaches to Students who are ELL				
Deficit-based --- Asset-based				
English only	Transitional bilingual education "early-exit"	Transitional bilingual education "late-exit"	Maintenance/ developmental bilingual education	Two-way bilingual education
Subtractive	Subtractive	Subtractive	Additive	Additive
Goal: English language development	Goal: English language development	Goal: English language development	Goal: Bilingualism	Goal: Bilingualism

Cornerstone 2: Establishing Equitable Structures in Educational Services

Second, Catholic schools must establish equitable structures in educational services for students who are ELL. Brisk (1998) addresses this topic by describing conditions of successful learning environments for these students. These conditions promote (a) language proficiency to academic grade level, (b) sociocultural integration to their ethnic community and the society at large, and (c) academic achievement as defined for all students. Catholic schools seeking to apply this cornerstone must structurally support these conditions. Brisk's first two points directly apply to this cornerstone of ICS, which focuses on equitable structures.

Brisk's (1998) first point, supporting language proficiency, begins with assessing and responding to students' levels of English proficiency. Language proficiency is determined by attending to the four language domains of listening, speaking, reading, and writing. The World-Class Instructional Design and Assessment (WIDA) Consortium (Gottlieb, 2004) defines these domains in the following manner:

1. *Listening*—process, understand, interpret, and evaluate spoken language in a variety of situations
2. *Speaking*—engage in oral communication in a variety of situations for an array of purposes and audiences
3. *Reading*—process, interpret, and evaluate written language, symbols and text with understanding and fluency
4. *Writing*—engage in written communication in a variety of forms for an array of purposes and audiences

These language proficiency levels can be charted on a scale to demonstrate the progression of language development, and these levels indicate how students who are ELL can be expected to perform (Gottlieb, 2004). These proficiency levels are illustrated in Table 4. By assessing levels of English language proficiency, schools can better determine how to support students who are ELL.

Brisk's (1998) second point is that schools must foster conditions for students who are English language learners to be socioculturally integrated. Catholic schools are poised to promote this integration when they keep to their philosophy that parents are the child's primary educators. This tenet, common to Catholic schools and aligned with the social teaching of subsidiarity, directs educators to reach out to the families of students who are ELL. Research shows that effective efforts to engage these families build on the "funds of knowledge" in homes (Moll & Gonzalez, 2004). A funds of knowledge approach directs educators to meet families in their homes and to explore the positive dynamics in their family structures. By visiting families of students who are ELL, Catholic school educators can begin to draw upon these dynamics, such as employment, family members' roles and responsibilities, hobbies, and cultural heritage. These efforts to integrate the families in a socially and culturally respectful manner lay the groundwork for reflecting on how the curriculum and school culture are inclusive and welcoming toward all members of the school community.

Table 4 *Performance Definitions for the K-12 English Language Proficiency Standards**	
English language proficiency level	At the given level of English language proficiency, English language learners will process, understand, produce, or use:
1 Entering	• pictorial or graphic representation of the language of the content areas; • words, phrases, or chunks of language when presented with one-step commands, directions, WH-questions, or statements with visual and graphic support
2 Beginning	• general language related to the content areas; • phrases or short sentences; • oral or written language with phonological, syntactic, or semantic errors that <u>often impede the meaning</u> of the communication when presented with one to multiple-step commands, directions, questions, or a series of statements with visual and graphic support
3 Developing	• general and some specific language of the content areas; • expanded sentences in oral interaction or written paragraphs; • oral or written language with phonological, syntactic, or semantic errors that <u>may impede the communication but retain much of its meaning</u> when presented with oral or written, narrative or expository descriptions with occasional visual and graphic support
4 Expanding	• specific and some technical language of the content areas; • a variety of sentence lengths of varying linguistic complexity in oral discourse or multiple, related paragraphs; • oral or written language with minimal phonological, syntactic, or semantic errors that <u>do not impede the overall meaning</u> of the communication when presented with oral or written connected discourse with occasional visual and graphic support
5 Bridging	• the technical language of the content areas; • a variety of sentence lengths of varying linguistic complexity in extended oral or written discourse, including stories, essays, or reports; • oral or written language approaching comparability to that of English proficient peers when presented with grade level material

Note. *Modified from WIDA's *English Language Proficiency Standards for English Language Learners in Kindergarten through Grade 12: Frameworks for Large-Scale State and Classroom Assessment Overview* (Gottlieb, 2004).

Cornerstone 3: Providing Access to High-Quality Teaching and Learning

Brisk's (1998) third point, that academic achievement as defined for all students must apply to students who are ELL, fits with the third cornerstone of ICS. By providing access to high-quality teaching and learning for all students, including those who are ELL, Catholic schools affirm the dignity of all students. Building the capacity of classroom teachers to serve these students is a key way for Catholic schools to pursue this.

Effective strategies for supporting English language learners in a general education setting are well established (Fillmore & Snow, 2000; Gibbons, 2002; Goldenberg, 2008; Short & Echevarria, 2004). Among these strategies, three fundamental orientations can guide general educators who are teaching students who are ELL (Goldenberg, 2008):

1. Support literacy in their home language, which promotes higher levels of reading achievement in English
2. Apply strong pedagogical methods and access to the general curriculum
3. Modify instruction to take into account students' language limitations

First, students who are ELL benefit when schools value their home language. When possible, students who are ELL should learn to read in their native language. Schools should support development of the home language, as this does not harm and often promotes English language proficiency (Slavin & Cheung, 2004, 2005). Reading proficiency in the language spoken at home is an important indicator of future performance in English (Garcia, 2000; Reese, Garnier, & Gallimore, 2000). Research by Reese et al. indicates that native-language literacy experiences support subsequent literacy development for students who are ELL. Literacy activities in one's home language contribute to English reading acquisition.

Second, students who are ELL are best served when they are exposed to strong pedagogical methods and provided access to the general curriculum. This is most likely to occur when they are integrated with other students. Lopez and Vazquez (2005) found that when students who are ELL are pulled out to work with English as a Second Language (ESL) experts, classroom teachers remain disconnected from the learning process of these children.

Third, students who are ELL benefit when teachers modify instruction to take into account their language limitations. Specifically, these students need support developing academic English. According to Scarcella (2003), "academic English is a variety or a register of English…characterized by the specific linguistic features associated with academic disciplines" (p. 9). The American Educational Research Association (2004) reports that academic English is the competence "to speak with confidence and comprehension in the classroom on academic subjects…includ[ing] the ability to read, write, and engage in substantive conversations about math, science, history, and other school subjects" (p. 2), and that students only develop this competence over several years. All students—both those who are ELL and those who are native speakers of English—must learn academic English. Often elementary students who are ELL learn to converse informally in English and pass as competent speakers while lagging behind classmates in academic English. Many problems of academic achievement by students who are ELL are rooted in deficiencies in academic English (Fillmore & Snow, 2000).

Academic English allows students to accomplish discipline-specific work. This needs to be taught to all students, but particularly to students who are ELL. Presenting a conceptual framework for understanding academic English, Scarcella (2003) argues "that there are regular features of academic English that are well defined and teachable" (p. 10). Literacy skills involve speaking, listening, reading, and writing, and are understood to encompass both basic decoding as well as higher-order skills such as conceptualizing, inferring, inventing, and testing (Fillmore & Snow, 2000). Fillmore and Snow report that students learn to speak, read, and write academic English primarily from teachers: "Teachers provide the help that students need to acquire this register when they go beyond discussions of content to discussions of the language used in texts for rhetorical and aesthetic effect" (p. 21).

In addition to attending to developing academic English, teachers need to be aware of other dynamics affecting participation and learning. For instance, students who are ELL are often more inhibited than their English proficient classmates to participate in classroom discussions (Verplaetse, 2000). Rieger and McGrail (2006) describe some of the reasons for such inhibition:

> Many English language learners struggle with feelings of inadequacy, fear of failure, low self-esteem and isolations. These feelings are associated with issues such as heavy accents that are mocked or ridiculed, grammatical errors in their oral speech, limited vocabulary, and lack of information about the social morays and behavior patterns in the classroom. (p. 5)

Deliberate strategies of ameliorating this include implementing a structured, predictable allotment of turns, or directly calling on the students who are ELL instead of waiting for them to volunteer. Teachers are encouraged and supported in developing such strategies when their schools' service delivery models emphasize that all students, including those who are ELL, belong first and foremost in heterogeneous classrooms with their peers. Social inclusion of students who are ELL has important connections to academic gains as well as other positive student outcomes (Kilman, 2009; Rieger & McGrail, 2006). In sum, simply including students who are ELL in general education classrooms does not guarantee their success. To ensure that they have access to high quality teaching and learning, this inclusion must be accompanied by specific pedagogical strategies and modifications.

A final component to providing high-quality teaching and learning is ensuring that the school has personnel who can serve both the students directly and be resources for all the educators in developing effective strategies of teaching students who are ELL. Schools with well-developed service delivery approaches for students who are ELL typically provide additional support personnel as bilingual teachers, English as a Second Language (ESL) teachers, and bilingual resource specialists. A bilingual teacher is a teacher who is literate in the home language of students who are ELL, and is typically certified as a teacher in bilingual education. An ESL teacher is a teacher who may not be able to speak the student's language at all, but has expertise in teaching students for whom English is not their first language. Many of the skills of an ESL teacher are similar to the skills of special education teachers. Typical strategies of ESL teachers include previewing the vocabulary of a lesson, using extensive visual aids to explain concepts and ideas, structuring the lesson to provide ample practice opportunities, and linking the lesson to the students' interests. Clearly the benefits of such strategies are not limited to students identified as ELL. A bilingual resource specialist is an educator without teacher certification who is literate in the home language of students who are ELL. Often these educators are from the community and serve as resources to ESL and classroom teachers, assisting monolingual educators with translation of materials, communication with students and families, and educational assistance within classrooms.

Cornerstone 4: Implementing Policy and Funding Mechanisms to Support Change
Finally, the fourth cornerstone of ICS directs schools to align funding and policy mechanisms within the service delivery model to support inclusion of all students. Clearly these two mechanisms are pivotal for Catholic schools striving to be inclusive toward students who are ELL. Absent funding mechanisms, intentions and plans for service delivery are merely noble ideas. Without policies that situate this service delivery into the broader teaching and learning community, these intentions and plans remain peripheral and tentative, not central and sustainable.

Funding mechanisms must support both recruitment and retention of students who are ELL. Recruiting these students requires identifying and ameliorating the barriers to their admission. One key barrier to admissions that many students who are ELL face in tuition-based Catholic schools is the cost (O'Keefe et al., 2004). The literature shows Catholic schools are successfully overcoming this barrier in numerous ways. Some schools have replaced tuition-dependent funding structures with alternate ones, such as the Nativity/Miguel (www.nativitymiguelschools.org) and Cristo Rey (www.cristoreynetwork.org) networks of schools. Some dioceses have replaced family-based tuitions with community-based support, using the stewardship model (Hamilton, 2008b). Publicly funded voucher schemes, pioneered in the cities of Milwaukee and Cleveland, are a third mechanism. While this has allowed some schools to stabilize and grow (Borsuk & Carr, 2005), vouchers are not showing themselves to be a panacea for urban Catholic schools serving students in poverty in general, or students who are ELL in particular (Hamilton, 2008b). Other successful strategies toward alternate funding mechanisms for Catholic schools include seeking privately-funded vouchers and developing extensive fundraising and marketing efforts through both new school personnel and focused school board committees (Haney & O'Keefe, 1999).

Alternative funding can make Catholic schools affordable and accessible for students who are ELL for whom tuition is a barrier. Funding mechanisms to support retention of these students are equally important. These include providing resources that support successful learning outcomes for these students. Such resources are those needed to enact the previous two cornerstones, namely equitable structures and high quality teaching and learning. For instance, structures that support language proficiency include assessment tools and personnel to administer them. Resources to support the sociocultural integration of students include funding to support teachers in making home-visits to families. Resources to support strong academic achievement for students who are ELL include professional development to build the capacity of teachers to support the development of academic English for these students. In short, funding resources that directly contribute to the success of students who are ELL is as important as addressing the initial barriers to admission that they face.

Along with implementing funding mechanisms to support inclusive service delivery for students who are ELL, Catholic school educators must ensure that policies are congruent as well. As described in chapter 4, school policies that affirm the Catholic social values of human dignity, the common good, and a preferential option for the marginalized will support ICS. To target policies specifically affecting students who are ELL, Catholic school leaders must critically analyze which policies are relevant to this population. At a basic level, does the school have any established policies guiding how it responds to students who are ELL? Is there a need to develop policies to guide teachers and administrators in making modifications and accommodations to curriculum, teaching, and assessment for these students? At the board level, are policies needed to ensure that strategic planning, development, and admissions efforts are taking into consideration the increasing linguistic pluralism in the community?

In this chapter I have attempted to extend the examination of inclusive service delivery beyond students with special needs to other dimensions of diversity. The four cornerstones of ICS provide Catholic schools a focus for specifically approaching inclusive service delivery in Catholic schools for students who are ELL. The use of Care Teams also provides a practical structure for Catholic schools to respond to the needs of all students who are struggling, regardless of the origins of these struggles. In the concluding chapter, we turn to consider how inclusive service delivery provides reasons for an optimistic view toward the future of Catholic education.

Conclusion

As I conclude this book, I return to Haugen's (1994) lyrics with which I began:

> Let us build a house where love can dwell
> And all can safely live,
> A place where saints and children tell
> How hearts learn to forgive.
>
> Built of hopes and dreams and visions,
> Rock of faith and vault of grace;
> Here the love of Christ shall end divisions;
> All are welcome, all are welcome,
> All are welcome in this place.

The future of Catholic schools is being paved by communities that are pursuing this vision, building on hopes and dreams and visions, and where love dwells and is expressed by welcoming all. All around the country Catholic school educators are struggling in this pursuit, striving to reduce barriers to students across multiple dimensions of diversity. In this book I have attempted to support this pursuit by providing a framework for inclusive service delivery grounded in the core values of Catholic social teaching (CST). Catholic elementary and secondary schools are guided by CST, which guides them to prioritize human dignity, the common good, and a preferential option for the marginalized.

In this book I have argued that CST compels Catholic schools to craft inclusive service delivery systems to effectively serve traditionally marginalized students. A consensus is emerging that Catholic schools are more authentic and aligned with CST to the degree that they serve traditionally marginalized students, but less cohesion exists around how to operationalize this. I have proposed that Catholic schools can do this by taking a systematic approach to developing inclusive service delivery. The model of Integrated Comprehensive Services (Frattura & Capper, 2007a) provides Catholic school leaders with a framework for such a systematic approach, and guides Catholic schools to welcome students across multiple dimensions of diversity.

Here I have emphasized specific dimensions of diversity that we typically associate with marginalization, such as special needs, linguistic differences, and poverty.

Examples abound, however, of other dimensions of diversity that affect how students experience schooling. For instance, students who are profoundly gifted are seldom served well in classrooms. They are frequently isolated, bored, and lonely. Students who are religious minorities in a community, living in non-traditional family structures, or lesbian, gay, bisexual or transgendered are just a few other examples of dimensions of diversity reflected in members of most school communities. The core values of Catholic social teaching form a compass for Catholic school leaders in navigating these waters in a manner that deepens and abides by the core identity of the school (Scanlan, 2008c).

A compass is a useful tool, but can only serve a traveler inclined to move. Weaver and Landers (2000) assert that educators' dispositions toward serving students who struggle are the primary barrier: "Opening the minds of educators remains one of our most difficult, and important, tasks" (p. 31). A systems-based approach to service delivery can play an important role in shifting dispositions in Catholic schools by presenting practical steps educators in these schools can take to implement change.

We are frequently inspired, provoked, and catalyzed to change our dispositions by disorienting dilemmas (Mezirow, 2000). Consider, for example, an anecdote familiar in all dioceses, and most schools: A family belongs to the parish. It is a stalwart supporter of the school, with two children attending. Then the family brings a third child to the school who presents a special need for which the school is unprepared. This poses a dilemma: How does the school respond to this child in an educationally appropriate manner (which might mean counseling them to another school), while at the same time being sensitive to the desire of the family to send all their children to the parish school? This dilemma triggers critical self-reflection, and frequently, changes in practices and policies. Mezirow argues that such disorienting dilemmas can promote transformative learning where habits of mind give way to alternative possibilities.

Catholic school educators navigating toward inclusive school communities may find themselves serving as positive deviants (Spreitzer & Sonenshein, 2004). Positive deviants are individuals who stray from the normal practices in manners that demonstrate new possibilities for improvement. Their deviancy demonstrates the unrealized potential that is latent within the organization. A Catholic school that effectively educates students with Down syndrome and autism spectrum disorders in inclusive settings serves as a positive deviant, allowing other Catholic school communities to imagine such transformation.

Signs of such positive deviants in Catholic school communities serving traditionally marginalized students are on the rise. Between 1989 and 1991 a National Congress on Catholic Schools for the 21st century, involving Catholic educators from around the United States, was held (Walch, 1996). Nineteen regional meetings culminated in a conference in Washington, DC. Out of the vision of this conference, a national Catholic educational dissemination system emerged in 1995. Boston College and the National Catholic Educational Association (NCEA) teamed up to create the Selected Programs for Improving Catholic Education network, dubbed SPICE (NCEA, 2009). The SPICE network, through an annual conference and publications, evaluates programs in Catholic schools and facilitates communication about effective ones. Each year exceptional programs that serve traditionally marginalized students have been featured, and some years the entire focus of the national conference is on Catholic social teaching (e.g., "Integrating the Social Teaching of the Church into Catholic Schools" in 2000, and "Catholic Schools for Children and Youth in Poverty" in 2003).

Positive deviants in Catholic schooling, forging inclusive school communities toward traditionally marginalized students, are grounded in their mission, and find resources to serve this mission. For instance, they build the skills of teachers to effectively teach students with learning disabilities. They forge relationships so that a child can receive occupational therapy in the classroom setting, and that the classroom teacher can make modifications to support this therapy. They hire bilingual staff and educate teachers in techniques to effectively engage linguistically diverse populations. Simply put, they walk the talk.

By contrast, many Catholic schools are increasingly grounded in a market-perspective, emphasizing the school's role in fostering economic and social mobility over religious, spiritual, and moral dimensions of the school (O'Keefe, 1999). O'Keefe points out that when Catholic schools are positioned by Catholics and non-Catholic parents alike within the metaphor of a marketplace of schools, then the "fundamental unit of consideration...is the individual...and not the well-being of the whole" (p. 20). This is a departure from what Grace (1996) refers to as the "distinctive educational mission and...historical educational commitments" (p. 70) of the schools. O'Keefe (1999) critiques the "many Catholic educators [who] uncritically embrace these [marketplace] principles, in practice and on the level of public policy" (p. 21). Elsewhere he is more direct: "The strength of Catholic schools is in mission, not margin" (O'Keefe, 1996, p. 192).

Grace (1996) argues that the market metaphor of education undermines Catholic schooling. He describes a "competitive market culture in schooling" (p. 70) as inimical to the traditional spiritual and moral values of Catholic schools:

> There is a fundamental tension, in the realm of education at least, between Catholic values and market values. Catholic values in education insist upon the primacy of spiritual, moral, and ethical understandings of the good life and of the good society. For Catholic education, academic achievement is not an end in itself but an enterprise serving a larger purpose. Catholic education cannot therefore operate as if pupils and students can be regarded as "inputs" and educational achievement regarded as "output." (p. 70)

Of course, as private schools, all Catholic schools must subscribe to the market metaphor at some level. If they do not attract students, they will close. Yet when the vision and values of Catholic schools are market-oriented, what distinguishes the

Catholic elementary schools from other private schools competing for students? Lower tuition rates, a religious curriculum, and strong classroom management might be characteristics that set these schools apart from other private schools. They might boast of higher student test scores, attendance rates, and graduation rates. But the distinguishing Catholic values that Grace (1996) describes are missing when a school is market-driven instead of mission-driven. Simply put, recruitment and retention practices aligned with marketing strategies are built from different premises than recruitment and retention practices rooted in the values of CST.

Martin (1996) predicts that the quality and relevance of Catholic schools in the 21st century will largely depend upon the degree to which they incorporate, affirm, and celebrate diversity. Catholic schools striving to embrace diversity by crafting inclusive systems of service delivery serve as lodestars. They are enacting the vision of inclusive Catholic education that was recently articulated in eloquent terms by the Holy See (Tomasi, 2008):

> [Inclusive] education is able to help forming individuals and new generations to social participation, to solidarity, to overcoming exclusion and to critically understand reality. At the same time an inclusive education involves a plurality of educational agencies and actors, all guided by the principle of subsidiarity that generates a synergy among family, teachers, professors and educators, young people themselves, non-governmental organizations, churches and religious communities and other persons that, in different ways, contribute to the formative process. While a more humane and inclusive society should care for the most vulnerable—and attention in educational policies to the right of the child is a significant aspect of this principle—school should constitute an environment in which educators could answer to the affective and cognitive needs of the child, not only in transmitting information, but also in being relevant for the children in this delicate phase of their lives. Then, educators should remain aware that they carry out their service in cooperation with parents, who are the first "educational agency" and have the priority right and duty to educate their children. This convergence of efforts is an evident application of the basic principle of subsidiarity.
>
> An inclusive education embraces all children and youth in their existential context and all persons dedicated to their formation, a comprehensive process that combines transmission of knowledge and development of personality. In fact, the fundamental questions any person asks deal with the search for meaning, of life and history, of change and dissolution, of love and transcendence. At its best, education provides everyone with the tools to contribute a creative participation in community, to reflect and give an appropriate answer to the unavoidable profound questions of meaning, to live with others, to discover one's nature and inherent dignity as spiritual creatures. (§3)

Truly Catholic schools strive to welcome all, following the adage of St. Benedict, to welcome all as Christ. They cannot do so haphazardly, building a robust teaching and learning community on the slippery ground of good intentions. Rather, they need to do so systematically and creatively, striving to attain the resources to continue to ameliorate the barriers. Diligence coupled with clear vision of a systematic approach to inclusive service delivery is essential. This will embolden Catholic schools to continue on the journey to build communities that affirm human dignity, serve the common good, and demonstrate a preferential option for the marginalized.

References

Alt, M. N., & Peter, K. (2002). *Private schools: A brief portrait*. Washington, DC: National Center for Education Statistics.

American Educational Research Association. (2004). English language learners: Boosting academic achievement. *AERA Research Points, 2*(1), 1-4.

Archdiocese of St. Louis Catholic Education Office. (2003a). *Implementing the learning consultant model for addressing students' special learning needs: A guidebook for schools* (2nd ed.). St. Louis, MO: Author.

Archdiocese of St. Louis Catholic Education Office. (2003b). *Resources for addressing students' special needs in Catholic schools and programs* (2nd ed.). St. Louis, MO: Author.

Archdiocese of St. Paul and Minneapolis, Office for Social Justice. (2006). *Key principles of Catholic social teaching*. Retrieved March 19, 2009, from http://www.osjspm.org/files/officeforsocialjustice/files/2%20page%20Catholic%20Social%20Teachings1.PDF

Artiles, A., Trent, S. C., & Palmer, J. D. (2004). Culturally diverse students in special education. In J. A. Banks & C. A. McGee Banks (Eds.), *Handbook of research on multicultural education* (2nd ed., pp. 716-735). San Francisco: Jossey-Bass.

Augenstein, J. (2003). NCEA's first century: An overview. In J. Augenstein, C. Kauffman, & R. Wister (Eds.), *One hundred years of Catholic education* (pp. 3-22). Washington, DC: National Catholic Educational Association.

Bahamonde, C., & Friend, M. (1999). Teaching English language learners: A proposal for effective service delivery. *Journal of Educational and Psychological Consultation, 10*(1), 1-24.

Bahr, M., & Kovaleski, J. (2006). The need for problem-solving teams. *Remedial and Special Education, 27*(1), 2-5.

Baker, D. (1999). Schooling all the masses: Reconsidering the origins of American schooling in the postbellum era. *Sociology of Education, 72*(4), 197-215.

Baker, D., & Riordan, C. (1998). The "eliting" of the common American Catholic school and the national education crisis. *Phi Delta Kappan, 80*(1), 16-23.

Baker, D., & Riordan, C. (1999). It's not about the failure of Catholic schools. *Phi Delta Kappan, 80*(6), 462-463.

Barton, J. (2000). "To include or not to include?" That is not the question. *Catholic Education: A Journal of Inquiry and Practice, 3*(3), 329-341.

Baynton, D. (2001). Disability and the justification of inequality in American history. In P. Longmore & L. Umansky (Eds.), *The new disability history: American perspectives* (pp. 33-57). New York: New York University Press.

Bedsworth, W., Colby, S., & Doctor, J. (2006). *Reclaiming the American dream*. New York: Bridgespan Group.

Belfield, C. (2003). *Democratic education across school types: Evidence from the NHES99*. New York: National Center for the Study of Privatization in Education.

Bello, D. (2004). *Issues facing Catholic high schools as they develop and implement inclusive practices for students with disabilities.* Unpublished doctoral dissertation, The George Washington University, Washington, DC.

Benton, J. L., & Owen, M. J. (1995). *Opening doors to people with disabilities* (Vol. 1). Washington, DC: National Catholic Office for Persons with Disabilities.

Benton, J. L., & Owen, M. J. (Eds.). (1997). *Opening doors to people with disabilities* (Vol. 2). Washington, DC: National Catholic Office for Persons with Disabilities.

Berliner, D. (2005). Our impoverished view of educational reform. *Teachers College Record, 108*(6), 949-995.

Bimonte, R. (2006). *Financing the mission: A profile of Catholic elementary schools in the United States 2005.* Washington, DC: National Catholic Educational Association.

Bishop, M. (1997). Inclusion: Balancing the ups and downs. In J. L. Benton & M. J. Owen (Eds.), *Opening doors to people with disabilities* (Vol. 1, pp. 1-5). Washington, DC: National Catholic Office for Persons with Disabilities.

Borsuk, A., & Carr, S. (2005, June 12). How is Milwaukee's experiment to expand school choice for low-income students faring 15 years later? *Milwaukee Journal Sentinal.* Retrieved February 26, 2009, from http://www.jsonline.com/news/metro/jun05/333144.asp

Brisk, M. E. (1998). *Bilingual education: From compensatory to quality schooling.* Mahwah, NJ: Lawrence Erlbaum.

Brotherson, M. J., Sheriff, G., Milburn, P., & Schertz, M. (2001). Elementary school principals and their needs and issues for inclusive early childhood programs. *Topics in Early Childhood Special Education, 21*(1), 31-45.

Broughman, S., & Swaim, N. (2006). *Characteristics of private schools in the United States: Results from the 2003-2004 private school universe survey.* Washington, DC: National Center for Education Statistics.

Brownell, M., Adams, A., Sindelar, P., Waldron, N. L., & Vanhover, S. (2006). Learning from collaboration: The role of teacher qualities. *Exceptional Children, 72*(2), 169-185.

Brown v. Board of Educ., 347 U.S. 483 (1954).

Bryk, A. (2000). Lessons from Catholic high schools on renewing our educational institutions. In T. McLaughlin, J. O'Keefe, & B. O'Keeffe (Eds.), *The contemporary Catholic school* (pp. 25-41). London: Falmer.

Bryk, A. (2009, January). *Catholic schools and the common good: Future directions and challenges.* Paper presented at the Catholic Higher Education Collaborative Conference, Los Angeles, CA.

Bryk, A., Lee, V., & Holland, P. (1993). *Catholic schools and the common good.* Cambridge, MA: Harvard University Press.

Buetow, H. (1988). *The Catholic school: Its roots, identity, and future.* New York: Crossroad.

Byron, W. (1999). Framing the principles of Catholic social thought. *Catholic Education: A Journal of Inquiry and Practice, 3*(1), 7-14.

Cambron-McCabe, N., & McCarthy, M. (2005). Educating school leaders for social justice. *Educational Policy, 19*(1), 201-222.

Capper, C., Frattura, E., & Keyes, M. (2000). *Meeting the needs of students of all abilities: How leaders go beyond inclusion.* Thousand Oaks, CA: Corwin Press.

Carr, J. (1997). Human dignity: The principle and the possibilities. *Momentum, 28*(3), 7-9.

Carrington, S., & Elkins, J. (2002). Bridging the gap between inclusive policy and inclusive culture in secondary schools. *Support for Learning, 17*(2), 51-57.

Cattaro, G. M. (2002). Catholic schools: Enduring presence in urban America. *Education and Urban Society, 35*(2), 100-110.

Chalfant, J. C., Pysh, M. V., & Moultrie, R. (1979). Teacher assistance teams: A model for within-building problem solving. *Learning Disability Quarterly, 2*(3), 95-96.

Chemerinsky, E. (2005). The segregation and resegregation of American public education: The court's role. In J. C. Boger & G. Orfield (Eds.), *School resegregation: Must the South turn back?* (pp. 26-47). Chapel Hill: University of North Carolina Press.

Coleman, J. (1991). Introduction: A tradition celebrated, reevaluated, and applied. In J. Coleman (Ed.), *One hundred years of Catholic social thought* (pp. 1-10). Maryknoll, NY: Orbis Books.

Coleman, J., & Hoffer, T. (1987). *Public and private schools: The impact of communities.* New York: Basic Books.

Coleman, J., Hoffer, T., & Kilgore, S. (1982). *High school achievement: Public, Catholic, and private compared.* New York: Basic Books.

Congregation for Catholic Education. (1977). *The Catholic school.* Homebush, NSW: Society of St. Paul.

Congregation for Catholic Education. (2007). *Educating together in Catholic schools: A shared mission between concecrated persons and the lay faithful.* Strathfield, NSW: St. Pauls.

Convey, J. (1992). *Catholic schools make a difference: Twenty-five years of research.* Washington, DC: National Catholic Educational Association.

Convey, J. (2008). Importance of leadership. In J. Staud (Ed.), *The Carnegie conversation on Catholic education* (pp. 28-30). Notre Dame, IN: Alliance for Catholic Education Press.

Cook, T., & Durow, W. P. (2008). The upper room: A university-archdiocesan partnership to develop leaders for Catholic schools. *Catholic Education: A Journal of Inquiry and Practice, 11*(3), 355-369.

Coons, S. (1997). Catholic schools serving disadvantaged students, Appendix C. *The Future of Children, 7*(3), 140-144.

Crawford, J. (2002). *Making sense of Census 2000.* Retrieved March 19, 2009, from http://www.language-policy.org/content/features/article5.htm

Crowley, A. L. W., & Wall, S. (2007). Supporting children with disabilities in the Catholic schools. *Catholic Education: A Journal of Inquiry and Practice, 10*(4), 508-522.

Cummins, J. (1986). Empowering minority students: A framework for intervention. *Harvard Educational Review, 56*(1), 18-36.

Curran, C. (2002). *Catholic social teaching, 1891-present: A historical, theological, and ethical analysis.* Washington, DC: Georgetown University Press.

Davis, C. (1990). *The history of Black Catholics in the United States.* New York: Crossroad.

DeFiore, L. (2006). The state of special education in Catholic schools. *Catholic Education: A Journal of Inquiry and Practice, 9*(4), 453-466.

Dorr, D. (1992). *Option for the poor: A hundred years of Vatican social teaching.* Dublin: Gill and MacMillan.

Doyle, M. (2004). Improving public policy advocacy through the effective use of data. *Catholic Education: A Journal of Inquiry and Practice, 8*(1), 69-85.

Drago-Severson, E. (2007). Helping teachers learn: Principals as professional development leaders. *Teachers College Record, 109*(1), 70-125.

Durow, W. P. (2007). Including and serving students with special needs in Catholic schools: A report of practices. *Catholic Education: A Journal of Inquiry and Practice, 10*(4), 473-489.

Durtschi, E. (2005). *Elementary school principals' involvement in special education: Roles, attitudes, and training.* Unpublished doctoral dissertation, University of Wisconsin, Madison.

Dykeman, B. (2006). Alternative strategies in assessing special education needs. *Education, 127*(2), 265-273.

Education for All Handicapped Children Act, Pub. L. No. 94-142 (1975).

The Education Trust. (2006). *Yes we can: Telling truths and dispelling myths about race and education in America.* Washington, DC: Author.

Elementary and Secondary Education Act, 20 U.S.C. §6301 et seq. (1965).

Equal Educational Opportunity Act, 20 U.S.C. §1703 (1974).

Fenzel, L. M., & Monteith, R. (2008). Successful alternative middle schools for urban minority children: A study of Nativity schools. *Journal of Education for Students Placed at Risk, 13*(4), 381-401.

Ferguson, D., Kozleski, E., Fulton, M. L., & Smith, A. (2005). *On... transformed, inclusive schools: A framework to guide fundamental change in urban schools.* Newton, MA: National Institute for Urban School Improvement. (ERIC Document Reproduction Service No. ED460172)

Ferri, B., & Connor, D. (2005). Tools of exclusion: Race, disability, and (re)segregated education. *Teachers College Record, 107*(3), 453-474.

Fillmore, L. W., & Snow, C. (2000). *What teachers need to know about language.* Washington, DC: Office of Educational Research and Improvement. (ERIC Document Reproduction Service No. ED444379)

Finn, C., & Petrilli, M. (2008). Foreword. In S. W. Hamilton (Ed.), *Who will save America's urban Catholic schools?* (pp. 7-11). New York: Thomas Fordham Institute.

Fitzgibbons, M., Mahon, M., & Maus, A. (2008). *The care team approach: A problem-solving process for effective school change.* Washington, DC: National Catholic Educational Association.

Fleming, D., Doerries, D., Stickney, D., & Spital, B. (2002, October). *Instructional support team initiative in Virginia.* Paper presented at the annual conference of the Virginia Psychological Association, Arlington, VA.

Frattura, E., & Capper, C. (2007a). *Leadership for social justice in practice: Integrated comprehensive services for all learners.* Thousand Oaks, CA: Corwin Press.

Frattura, E., & Capper, C. (2007b). New teacher teams to support integrated comprehensive services. *Teaching Exceptional Children, 39*(4), 16-22.

Fullan, M. (2004). *Leadership and sustainability: System thinkers in action.* Thousand Oaks, CA: Corwin Press.

Fullan, M. (2006). The future of educational change: System thinkers in action. *Journal of Educational Change, 7*(3), 113-122.

Garcia, G. (2000). Bilingual children's reading. In M. L. Kamil, P. B. Mosenthal, P. D. Pearson, & R. Barr (Eds.), *Handbook of reading research* (Vol. 3, pp. 813-834). Mahwah, NJ: Erlbaum.

Gibbons, P. (2002). *Scaffolding language, scaffolding learning: Teaching second language learners in the mainstream classroom.* Portsmouth, NH: Heinemann.

Goldenberg, C. (2008). Teaching English language learners: What the research does—and does not—say. *American Educator, 32*(2), 8-23, 42-44.

Gottlieb, M. (2004). *English language proficiency standards for English language learners in kindergarten through Grade 12.* Madison, WI: World-Class Instructional Design and Assessment Consortium.

Grace, G. (1996). Leadership in Catholic schools. In T. McLaughlin, J. O'Keefe, & B. O'Keeffe (Eds.), *The contemporary Catholic school: Context, identity, and diversity* (pp. 70-88). Washington, DC: Falmer.

Grace, G. (2002). *Catholic schools: Mission, markets, and morality*. London: Routledge/Falmer.

Gravois, T., & Rosenfield, S. (2006). Impact of instructional consultation teams on the disproportionate referral and placement of minority students in special education. *Remedial and Special Education, 27*(3), 42-52.

Gray, M., & Gautier, M. (2006). *Primary trends, challenges, and outlook: A report on U.S. Catholic elementary schools 2000-2005*. Washington, DC: National Catholic Educational Association.

Greene, J. P., Peterson, P. E., & Du, J. (1998). School choice in Milwaukee: A randomized experiment. In P. E. Peterson & B. Hassel (Eds.), *Learning from school choice* (pp. 335-356). Washington, DC: Brookings Press.

Griffin v. County School Board, 377 U.S. 218 (1964).

Groome, T. (1998). *Educating for life*. Allen, TX: Thomas More.

Guerra, M. (2000). Key issues for the future of Catholic schools. In T. Hunt, T. Oldenski, & T. Wallace (Eds.), *Catholic school leadership: An invitation to lead* (pp. 79-90). New York: Falmer.

Hale, J. B., Kaufman, A., Naglieri, J. A., & Kavale, K. A. (2006). Implementation of IDEA: Integrating response to intervention and cognitive assessment methods. *Psychology in the Schools, 43*(7), 753-770.

Hamilton, S. W. (2008a). Introduction. In S. W. Hamilton (Ed.), *Who will save America's urban Catholic schools?* (pp. 12-20). New York: Thomas Fordham Institute.

Hamilton, S. W. (Ed.). (2008b). *Who will save America's urban Catholic schools?* New York: Thomas Fordham Institute.

Haney, R., & O'Keefe, J. (1999). *Creatively financing and resourcing Catholic schools*. Washington, DC: National Catholic Educational Association.

Harris, C. R., Kaff, M. S., Anderson, M. J., & Knackendoffel, A. (2007). Designing flexible instruction. *Principal Leadership, 7*(9), 31-35.

Hartman, W., & Fay, T. (1996). *Cost-effectiveness of instructional support teams in Pennsylvania* (Policy paper). Palo Alto, CA: Center for Special Education Finance.

Haugen, M. (Composer). (1994). All are welcome. On *All are welcome* [CD]. Chicago: GIA Publications. (1995)

Hoffer, T. (2000). Catholic school attendance and student achievement: A review and extension of research. In J. Youniss & J. Convey (Eds.), *Catholic schools at the crossroads: Survival and transformation* (pp. 87-112). New York: Teachers College Press.

Hoffer, T., Greeley, A., & Coleman, J. (1985). Achievement growth in public and Catholic schools. *Sociology of Education, 58*(2), 74-97.

Holland, J., & Henriot, P. (1983). *Social analysis: Linking faith and justice*. Maryknoll, NY: Orbis Books.

Hollenbach, D. (1996). The common good, pluralism, and Catholic education. In T. McLaughlin, J. O'Keefe, & B. O'Keeffe (Eds.), *The contemporary Catholic school: Context, identity, and diversity* (pp. 89-103). Washington, DC: Falmer.

Holy See. (2000). *Catechism of the Catholic Church* (2nd ed.). Washington, DC: United States Catholic Conference.

Hornsby-Smith, M. (2006). *An introduction to Catholic social thought*. New York: Cambridge University Press.

Hunt, T. (2000). The history of Catholic schools in the United States: An overview. In T. Hunt, T. Oldenski, & T. Wallace (Eds.), *Catholic school leadership: An invitation to lead* (pp. 34-58). New York: Falmer.

Hunt, T., Oldenski, T., & Wallace, T. (Eds.). (2000). *Catholic school leadership: An invitation to lead*. New York: Falmer.

Individuals with Disabilities Education Act, 20 U.S.C. §1400 et seq. (2004).

Jacobs, R. (1998a). U.S. Catholic schools and the religious who served in them: Contributions in the 18th and 19th centuries. *Catholic Education: A Journal of Inquiry and Practice, 1*(4), 364-383.

Jacobs, R. (1998b). U.S. Catholic schools and the religious who served in them: Contributions in the first six decades of the 20th century. *Catholic Education: A Journal of Inquiry and Practice, 2*(1), 15-34.

Jacobs, R. (1998c). U.S. Catholic schools and the religious who served in them: The struggle to continue the tradition in the post-Vatican II era. *Catholic Education: A Journal of Inquiry and Practice, 2*(2), 159-176.

John Paul II. (1995). *Evangelium vitae* [Gospel of life]. New York: Random House.

Johnson, D. W., & Johnson, F. P. (2009). *Joining together: Group theory and group skills* (10th ed.). Needham Heights, MA: Allyn & Bacon.

Johnson, R. S. (2002). *Using data to close the achievement gap: How to measure equity in our schools*. Thousand Oaks, CA: Corwin Press.

Kantor, H., & Lowe, R. (2006). From New Deal to no deal: No Child Left Behind and the devolution of responsibility for equal opportunity. *Harvard Educational Review, 76*(4), 474-502.

Kilman, C. (2009). Lonely language learners. *Teaching Tolerance, 35*(Spring). Retrieved March 19, 2009, from http://www.tolerance.org/teach/magazine/index.jsp#

Kovaleski, J., Gickling, E., Morrow, H., & Swank, P. (1999). High versus low implementation of instructional support teams: A case for maintaining program fidelity. *Remedial and Special Education, 20*(3), 170-183.

Kovaleski, J., Tucker, J., & Stevens, L. (1996). Bridging special and regular education: The Pennsylvania Initiative. *Educational Leadership, 53*(5), 44-47.

Kugelmass, J. (2004). *The inclusive school: Sustaining equity and standards*. New York: Teachers College Press.

Lawrence, S. (2000). "New" immigrants in the Catholic schools: A preliminary analysis. In J. Youniss & J. Convey (Eds.), *Catholic schools at the crossroads: Survival and transformation* (pp. 178-200). New York: Teachers College Press.

Lawrence-Brown, D., & Muschaweck, K. (2004). Getting started with collaborative teamwork for inclusion. *Catholic Education: A Journal of Inquiry and Practice, 8*(2), 146-161.

Lee, V., Chow-Hoy, T., Burkam, D., Geverdt, D., & Smerdon, B. (1998). Sector differences in high school course taking: A private school or Catholic school effect? *Sociology of Education, 71*(4), 314-336.

Lefevere, P. (2005, March 25). Program celebrates uniqueness. *National Catholic Reporter*, pp. 6A, 11A.

Leo XIII. (1891). *Rerum novarum* [On the condition of labor]. Philadelphia: Hardy & Mahony.

Lipsky, D. K., & Gartner, A. (1996). Inclusion, school restructuring, and the remaking of American society. *Harvard Educational Review, 66*(4), 762-797.

Long, T., Brown, C., & Nagy-Rado, A. (2007). Preparing special educators to assume collaborative and consultative roles. *Catholic Education: A Journal of Inquiry and Practice, 10*(4), 409-507.

Long, T., & Schuttloffel, M. J. (2006). A rationale for special education in Catholic schools. *Catholic Education: A Journal of Inquiry and Practice, 9*(4), 443-452.

Lopez, G. R. (2001). The value of hard work: Lessons on parent involvement from an (im)migrant household. *Harvard Educational Review, 71*(3), 416-437.

Lopez, G. R., Scribner, J. D., & Mahitivanichcha, K. (2001). Redefining parental involvement: Lessons from high-performing migrant-impacted schools. *American Educational Research Journal, 38*(2), 253-288.

Lopez, G. R., & Vazquez, V. (2005, November). *"They don't speak English": Interrogating racist ideologies and perceptions of school personnel in a Midwestern state.* Paper presented at the national conference of University Council for Educational Administration, Nashville, TN.

Losen, D., & Welner, K. (2001). Disabling discrimination in our public schools: Comprehensive legal challenges to inappropriate and inadequate special education services for minority children. *Harvard Civil Rights-Civil Liberties Law Review, 36*(2), 407-460.

Lummert, N. (2000). *Children on the move: The plight of immigrant and refugee children.* Washington, DC: United States Catholic Conference, Migration and Refugee Services.

Martin, C. D. (Lyricist), & Gabriel, C. (Composer). (1905). His eye is on the sparrow [Recorded by Mahalia Jackson]. On *Gospels, spirituals, and hymns* [CD]. New York: Sony. (1991)

Martin, S. (1996). *Cultural diversity in Catholic schools.* Washington, DC: National Catholic Educational Association.

Martin, S., & Litton, E. (2004). *Equity, advocacy and diversity: New directions for Catholic schools.* Washington, DC: National Catholic Educational Association.

Martinez, R., Nellis, L., & Prendergast, K. (2006). Closing the achievement gap series: Part II. Response-to-intervention (RTI)—Basic elements, practical applications, and policy recommendations. *Center for Evaluation & Education Policy Brief, 4*(8), 1-6.

Mawdsley, R. D. (2000). *Legal problems of religious and private schools* (4th ed.). Dayton, OH: Education Law Association.

McCullough, M., Graf, V., Leung, B., Stroud, M., & Orlando, M. (2008). *Building community through school success teams.* Washington, DC: National Catholic Educational Association.

McDonald, D. (2005). Federal education law and private school children: Key concepts to opening equitable participation doors. *Momentum, 36*(3), 102-103.

McDonald, D. (2007a). Making education law work for Catholic schools. *Momentum, 38*(1), 96-97.

McDonald, D. (2007b, July). *Update on federal education policy and legislation.* Paper presented at the fifth annual Education Law Symposium, Louisville, KY.

McDonald, D., & Schultz, M. (2008). *United States Catholic elementary and secondary schools 2007-2008: The annual statistical report on schools, enrollment, and staffing.* Washington, DC: National Catholic Educational Association.

McEwan, P. (2000). *Comparing the effectiveness of public and private schools: A review of evidence and interpretations* (Occasional Paper No. 3). New York: National Center for the Study of Privatization in Education, Teachers College.

McGreevy, J. (2003). *Catholicism and American freedom: A history.* New York: W.W. Norton.

McLaughlin, D. (2000). The Catholic school: Avenue to authenticity. *Momentum, 3*(3), 274-292.

McLeskey, J., & Waldron, N. L. (2000). *Inclusive schools in action.* Alexandria, VA: Association for Supervision and Curriculum Development.

Mezirow, J. (2000). Learning to think like an adult: Core concepts of transformational theory. In J. Mezirow & Associates (Eds.), *Learning as transformation: Critical perspectives on a theory in progress* (pp. 3-33). San Francisco: Jossey-Bass.

Moll, L., & Gonzalez, N. (2004). Engaging life: A funds-of-knowledge approach to multicultural education. In J. A. Banks & C. A. M. Banks (Eds.), *Handbook of research on multicultural education* (pp. 699-715). San Francisco: John Wiley & Sons.

Moore, C. (2003). Ethnicity and parish schools: African Americans. In J. Augenstein, C. Kauffman, & R. Wister (Eds.), *One hundred years of Catholic education* (pp. 241-256). Washington, DC: National Catholic Educational Association.

Morris, C. R. (1997). *American Catholic: The saints and sinners who built America's most powerful church.* New York: Times Books.

National Association of State Directors of Special Education & Council of Administrators of Special Education. (2006). *Response to intervention* (White paper). Alexandria, VA: Author.

National Catholic Educational Association. (2009). *Selected programs for improving Catholic education.* Retrieved February 23, 2009, from http://www.ncea.org/services/SPICE.asp

National Center for Education Statistics. (2002). *Private school universe survey.* Retrieved March 19, 2009, from http://nces.ed.gov/surveys/pss/tables.asp

National Center for Education Statistics. (2004). *Language minorities and their educational and labor market indicators: Recent trends.* Washington, DC: U.S. Department of Education.

National Conference of Catholic Bishops. (1972). To teach as Jesus did. *Origins, 6*(1), 1-7.

National Conference of Catholic Bishops. (1986). *Economic justice for all: Catholic social teaching and the U.S. economy.* Washington, DC: United States Conference of Catholic Bishops.

National Conference of Catholic Bishops. (1989). *Pastoral statement of U.S. Catholic bishops on people with disabilities.* Washington, DC: Author.

National Conference of Catholic Bishops. (1993). *Communities of salt and light: Reflections on the social mission of the parish.* Washington, DC: United States Catholic Conference.

National Conference of Catholic Bishops. (1995). *Guidelines for the celebration of the sacraments with people with disabilities.* Washington, DC: Author.

National Conference of Catholic Bishops. (1998a). *Summary report of the task force on Catholic social teaching and Catholic education.* Washington, DC: United States Catholic Conference.

National Conference of Catholic Bishops. (1998b). *Welcome and justice for persons with disabilities.* Washington, DC: Author.

National Council on Disability. (2000). *Back to school on civil rights.* Washington, DC: Author.

O'Collins, G., Kendall, D., & LaBelle, J. (Eds.). (2007). *Pope John Paul II: A reader.* Mahwah, NJ: Paulist Press.

O'Keefe, J. (1996). No margin, no mission. In T. McLaughlin, J. O'Keefe & B. O'Keeffe (Eds.), *The contemporary Catholic school: Context, identity, and diversity* (pp. 177-197). Washington, DC: Falmer.

O'Keefe, J. (1999). Visionary leadership in Catholic schools. In J. Conroy (Ed.), *Catholic education inside-out/outside-in* (pp. 15-38). Dublin: Veritas.

O'Keefe, J. (2000). Leadership in urban elementary schools. In T. Hunt, T. Oldenski, & T. Wallace (Eds.), *Catholic school leadership: An invitation to lead* (pp. 225-243). New York: Falmer.

O'Keefe, J., & Evans, M. P. (2004). *Catholic education: A call to serve the poor.* Washington, DC: National Catholic Educational Association.

O'Keefe, J., Greene, J., Henderson, S., Connors, M., Goldschmidt, E., & Schervish, K. (2004). *Sustaining the legacy: Inner-city Catholic elementary schools in the United States.* Washington, DC: National Catholic Educational Association.

O'Keefe, J., & Murphy, J. (2000). Ethnically diverse Catholic schools: School structure, students, staffing, and finance. In J. Youniss & J. Convey (Eds.), *Catholic schools at the crossroads: Survival and transformation* (pp. 117-136). New York: Teachers College Press.

Olneck, M. (2004). Immigrants and education in the United States. In C. A. M. Banks & J. A. Banks (Eds.), *Handbook of research on multicultural education* (2nd ed., pp. 381-403). San Francisco: Jossey-Bass.

Orfield, G. (2001). *Schools more separate: Consequences of a decade of resegregation.* Cambridge, MA: Harvard University, The Civil Rights Project.

Orfield, G., & Lee, C. (2005). *Why segregation matters: Poverty and educational inequality.* Cambridge, MA: Harvard University, The Civil Rights Project.

Orfield, G., & Lee, C. (2007). *Historical reversals, accelerating resegregation, and the need for new integration strategies.* Los Angeles, CA: Civil Rights Project/Proyecto Derechos Civiles, UCLA.

O'Shea, D., & O'Shea, L. (1998). Learning to include: Lessons learned from a high school without special education services. *Teaching Exceptional Children, 31*(2), 40-48.

Ovando, C. (2003). Bilingual education in the United States: Historical development and current issues. *Bilingual Research Journal, 27*(1), 1-25.

Owen, M. J. (1988, May). *Persons with disabilities.* Paper presented at the Catholic Education Futures Project Symposium, Dayton, OH.

Owen, M. J. (1997). Catholic education and students with disabilities: Historical perspectives and future visions. In J. L. Benton & M. J. Owen (Eds.), *Opening doors* (Vol. 2, pp. 1-9). Washington, DC: National Catholic Office for Persons with Disabilities.

Owen, M. J. (2002). Demographics of disability. *The Priest, 59*(7), 20-22.

Owens, R. F. (2005). Urban revitalization: A case study of one Catholic elementary school's journey. *Catholic Education: A Journal of Inquiry and Practice, 9*(1), 58-74.

Paul VI. (1967). *Populorum progressio* [On the development of peoples]. Washington, DC: United States Catholic Conference.

Pisha, B., & Coyne, P. (2001). Smart from the start. *Remedial and Special Education, 22*(4), 197-203.

Plessy v. Ferguson, 163 U.S. 537 (1896).

Polite, V. (1992). Getting the job done well: African American students and Catholic schools. *Journal of Negro Education, 61*(2), 211-222.

Polite, V. (2000). Cornerstones: Catholic high schools that serve predominantly African American populations. In J. Youniss & J. Convey (Eds.), *Catholic schools at the crossroads: Survival and transformation* (pp. 137-156). New York: Teachers College Press.

Pontifical Council for Justice and Peace. (2004). *Compendium of the social doctrine of the Church.* Vatican City: Libreria Editrice Vaticana.

Powell, M. (2004). Catholic high schools: Can inclusion work without significant publicly-funded resources? *Catholic Education: A Journal of Inquiry and Practice, 8*(1), 86-106.

Praisner, C. (2003). Attitudes of elementary school principals toward the inclusion of students with disabilties. *Exceptional Children, 69*(2), 135-145.

Prasse, D. (2006). Legal supports for problem-solving systems. *Remedial and Special Education, 27*(1), 7-15.

Prater, M. A. (2003). She will succeed! *Teaching Exceptional Children, 35*(5), 58-64.

President's Commission on Excellence in Special Education. (2002). *A new era: Revitalizing special education for children and their families.* Washington, DC: Author.

Pugach, M., & Warger, C. L. (2001). Curriculum matters. *Remedial and Special Education, 22*(4), 194-196.

Rea, P., McLaughlin, V., & Walther-Thomas, C. (2002). Outcomes for students with learning disabilities in inclusive and pullout programs. *Exceptional Children, 68*(2), 203-222.

Reese, L., Garnier, H., & Gallimore, R. (2000). Longitudinal analysis of the antecedents of emergent Spanish literacy and middle-school English reading achievement of Spanish-speaking students. *American Educational Research Journal, 37*(3), 633-662.

Rehabilitation Act of 1973, 29 U.S.C. §§791-794 (1998).

Reid, D. K., & Valle, J. W. (2004). The discursive practice of learning disability: Implications for instruction and parent-school relations. *Journal of Learning Disabilities, 37*(6), 466-482.

Rieger, A., & McGrail, E. (2006). *Understanding English language learners' needs and the language acquisition process: Two teacher educators' perspectives.* Tempe, AZ: National Institute for Urban School Improvement.

Riordan, C. (2000). Trends in student demography in Catholic secondary schools, 1972-1992. In J. Youniss & J. Convey (Eds.), *Catholic schools at the crossroads: Survival and transformation* (pp. 33-54). New York: Teachers College Press.

Rose, D., & Meyer, A. (2002). *Teaching every student in the digital age: Universal design for learning.* Alexandria, VA: Association for Supervision and Curriculum Development.

Rosenfield, S. (1987). *Instructional consultation.* Hillsdale, NJ: Erlbaum.

Russo, C. J., Massucci, J. D., & Osborne, A. G. (2000). The delivery of special education services in Catholic schools: One hand gives, the other hand takes away. *Catholic Education: A Journal of Inquiry and Practice, 3*(3), 375-389.

Russo, C. J., Massucci, J. D., Osborne, A. G., & Cattaro, G. M. (2002). *Catholic schools and the law of special education: A reference guide.* Washington, DC: National Catholic Educational Association.

Salisbury, D. (2003). *Lessons from Florida: School choice gives increased opportunities to children with special needs* (Briefing Paper No. 81). Washington, DC: Cato Institute.

Sander, W. (1996). Catholic grade schools and academic achievement. *Journal of Human Resources, 31*(3), 540-548.

Sander, W. (2001). *Catholic schools: Private and social effects.* Boston: Kluwer Academic Publishers.

Sanders, J. (1977). *The education of an urban minority: Catholics in Chicago, 1833–1965.* New York: Oxford University Press.

Scanlan, M. (2006a, April). *Grammar of Catholic schooling and radically "catholic" schools.* Paper presented at the annual meeting of the American Educational Research Association, San Francisco.

Scanlan, M. (2006b). Problematizing the pursuit of social justice education. *UCEA Review, XLV*(3), 6-8.

Scanlan, M. (2008a). Caregiver engagement in religious urban elementary schools. *Marriage & Family Review, 43*(2), 308-337.

Scanlan, M. (2008b, March). *Encouraging and discouraging Catholic schools from serving students with special needs in inclusive environments.* Paper presented at the annual meeting of the American Educational Research Association, New York.

Scanlan, M. (2008c). Grammar of Catholic schooling and radically "catholic" schools. *Catholic Education: A Journal of Inquiry and Practice, 12*(1), 25-54.

Scanlan, M. (in press-a). Emerging trends of inclusive Catholic schools. In P. Bauch & T. Hunt (Eds.), *Catholic schools in the public interest: Past, present, future.* Charlotte, NC: Information Age Publishers.

Scanlan, M. (in press-b). Moral, legal, and functional dimensions of inclusive service delivery in Catholic schools. *Catholic Education: A Journal of Inquiry and Practice.*

Scarcella, R. (2003). *Academic English: A conceptual framework* (Technical Report No. 2003-1). Irvine: University of California Linguistic Minority Research Institute.

Scheurich, J. J., & Skrla, L. (2003). *Leadership for equity and excellence: Creating high-achievement classrooms, schools, and districts.* Thousand Oaks, CA: Corwin Press.

Schuck, M. (1991). *That they be one: The social teaching of the papal encyclicals, 1740-1989.* Washington, DC: Georgetown University Press.

Schuttloffel, M. J. (2003). *Report on the future of Catholic school leadership.* Washington, DC: National Catholic Educational Association.

Schuttloffel, M. J. (2008). *Contemplative leadership that creates a culture of continuous improvement.* Washington, DC: National Catholic Educational Association.

Shaughnessy, M. A. (2005). *The law and Catholic schools: A guide to legal issues for the third millennium* (2nd ed.). Washington, DC: National Catholic Educational Association.

Short, D., & Echevarria, J. (2004). Teacher skills to support English language learners. *Educational Leadership, 62*(4), 8-13.

Sindelar, P., Shearer, D. K., Yendol-Hoppey, D., & Liebert, T. (2006). The sustainability of inclusive school reform. *Exceptional Children, 72*(3), 317-331.

Slavin, R. E., & Cheung, A. (2004). How do English language learners learn to read? *Educational Leadership, 61*(6), 52-57.

Slavin, R. E., & Cheung, A. (2005). A synthesis of research on language of reading instruction for English language learners. *Review of Educational Research, 75*(2), 247-284.

Smith-Maddox, R., & Wheelock, A. (1995). Untracking and students' futures. *Phi Delta Kappan, 77,* 222-229.

Spreitzer, G. M., & Sonenshein, S. (2004). Toward the construct definition of positive deviance. *American Behavioral Scientist, 47*(6), 828-847.

Spring, J. (1989). *The sorting machine revisited: National educational policy since 1945.* New York: Longman.

Stevens-Arroyo, A., & Pantoja, S. (2003). History and inculturation: The Latino experience of Catholic education. In J. Augenstein, C. Kauffman, & R. Wister (Eds.), *One hundred years of Catholic education* (pp. 257-281). Washington, DC: National Catholic Educational Association.

Storz, M., & Nestor, K. (2007). *They call us to justice: Responding to the call of the Church and our students.* Washington, DC: National Catholic Educational Association.

Stout, K. S. (2001). *Special education inclusion.* Retrieved March 19, 2009, from http://www.weac.org/resource/june96/speced.htm

TASH. (2000). *TASH Resolution on inclusive quality education.* Retrieved October 13, 2005, from http://www.tash.org/IRR/resolutions/res02inclusiveed.htm

Taylor, S. (1988). Caught in the continuum: A critical analysis of the principle of the least restrictive environment. *Journal of the Association for Persons with Severe Handicaps, 13*(1), 41-53.

Taylor, S. (2001). The continuum and current controversies in the USA. *Journal of Intellectual and Developmental Disability, 26*(1), 15-33.

Theoharis, G. (2007). Social justice educational leaders and resistance: Toward a theory of social justice leadership. *Educational Administration Quarterly, 43*(2), 221-258.

Thomas, W., & Collier, V. (2001). *A national study of school effectiveness for language minority students' long-term academic achievement.* Washington, DC: Center for Research on Education, Diversity, and Excellence.

Thousand, J., Villa, R., & Nevin, A. (2006). The many faces of collaborative planning and teaching. *Theory into Practice, 45*(3), 239-248.

Tomasi, S. (2008, November). *Provides everyone with the tools to contribute.* Paper presented at the United Nations 48th International Conference on Education, Geneva.

Tomlinson, C. A., & Allan, S. D. (2000). *Leadership for differentiating schools and classrooms.* Alexandria, VA: Association for Supervision and Curriculum Development.

Tomlinson, C. A., & McTighe, J. (2006). *Integrating differentiated instruction and understanding by design: Connecting content and kids.* Alexandria, VA: Association for Supervision and Curriculum Development.

Turnbull, A., Turnbull, R., Shank, M., & Smith, S. J. (2003). *Exceptional lives: Special education in today's schools* (4th ed.). Upper Saddle River, NJ: Prentice Hall.

Tyack, D., & Tobin, W. (1994). The "grammar" of schooling: Why has it been so hard to change? *American Educational Research Journal, 31*(3), 453-479.

United States Conference of Catholic Bishops. (2002). *Catholic school children with disabilities.* Washington, DC: Author.

United States Conference of Catholic Bishops. (2005a). *Renewing our commitment to Catholic elementary and secondary schools in the third millennium.* Washington, DC: Author.

United States Conference of Catholic Bishops. (2005b). *Themes of Catholic social teaching.* Retrieved March 19, 2009, from http://www.usccb.org/sdwp/projects/socialteaching/excerpt.shtml

U.S. Department of Education. (2003). *Number of children served under IDEA, Part B by age group, during the 2002-03 school year.* Retrieved March 19, 2009, from http://www.ideadata.org/tables26th/ar_aa1.htm

Valenzuela, J. S. D., Copeland, S., Qi, C. H., & Park, M. (2006). Examining educational equity: Revisiting the disproportionate representation of minority students in special education. *Exceptional Children, 72*(4), 425-441.

Vallely, P. (Ed.). (1998). *The new politics: Catholic social teaching for the twenty-first century.* London: SCM Press.

Vatican Council II. (1965a). *Gaudium et spes* [On the church in the modern world]. Boston: St. Paul.

Vatican Council II. (1965b). *Gravissimum educationis* [On Christian education]. Washington, DC: National Catholic Welfare Conference.

Verplaetse, L. S. (2000). How content teachers allocate turns to limited English proficient students. *Journal of Education, 182*(3), 19-35.

Villa, R., Thousand, J., Meyers, H., & Nevin, A. (1996). Teacher and administrator perceptions of heterogeneous education. *Exceptional Children, 63*(1), 29-48.

Walch, T. (1996). *Parish school: American Catholic parochial education from colonial times to the present.* New York: Crossroad.

Ware, L. (2002). A moral conversation on disability: Risking the personal in educational contexts. *Hypatia, 17*(3), 143-174.

Ware, L. (Ed.). (2004). *Ideology and the politics of (in)exclusion.* New York: Peter Lang

Warren, G. S. (1997). *Ev'ry time I feel the spirit: 101 best-loved psalms, gospel hymns, and spiritual songs of the African-American church* (1st ed.). New York: Henry Holt.

Weaver, R., & Landers, M. F. (2000). Our vocation: To serve all. *Momentum, 31*(3), 28-31.

Whitfield, T. J. (1996). *Academic effectiveness of Allegheny County middle schools' instructional support teams.* (ERIC Document Reproduction Service No. ED412580)

Winzer, M. (1993). *The history of special education: From isolation to integration.* Washington, DC: Gallaudet University Press.

World Synod of Catholic Bishops. (1971). *Justice in the world.* Vatican City: Typis Polyglottis Vaticanis.

About the Author

 **Martin K. Scanlan**, Ph.D., is an assistant professor in the Department of Educational Policy and Leadership in the College of Education at Marquette University. His principal area of scholarship examines how school leaders can more effectively cultivate school communities that serve traditionally marginalized students. His current research projects focus on schools and school systems reforming their service delivery for students with special needs and students who are English language learners. He received his Ph.D. from the Department of Educational Policy and Leadership Analysis in the College of Education at the University of Wisconsin, Madison. Before joining Marquette, Scanlan spent over a decade as a teacher and administrator in Catholic elementary schools in Washington, DC, Berkeley, CA, and Madison, WI. He remains an active member of the Catholic educational community, serving on a local high school board and regularly collaborating with local, regional, and national school leaders.

CPSIA information can be obtained
at www.ICGtesting.com
Printed in the USA
FSHW01n1954090818
51312FS